FINANCIAL TIMES
Management Briefings

Measuring Managerial and Business Performance

RICHARD PETTINGER

PITMAN PUBLISHING

London • Hong Kong • Johannesburg • Melbourne • Singapore • Washington DC

PITMAN PUBLISHING
128 Long Acre, London WC2E 9AN
Tel: +44 (0)171 447 2000
Fax: +44 (0)171 240 5771

A Division of Pearson Professional Limited

First published in Great Britain 1997

ISBN 0 273 63186 1

British Library Cataloguing in Publication Data
A CIP catalogue record for this book can be obtained from the British Library.

10 9 8 7 6 5 4 3 2 1

Printed and bound in Great Britain

The Publishers' policy is to use paper manufactured from sustainable forests.

Contents

Preface v

About the author vi

1   **Introduction** 1
     Prerequisites for successful and effective performance . . . 2
     Components of successful performance 3
     Information 5
     Responsibilities 6
     Aims and objectives 10
     Conclusions 13

2   **Qualitative measures of performance** 14
     Introduction 14
     Priorities 15
     Objectives 16
     Motivation 17
     Performance appraisal 21
     Occupational health 23
     Pay, remuneration and reward 25
     Ethics 27
     Administration 29
     Conclusions 30

3   **Quantitative aspects of performance** 32
     Introduction 32
     Finance 33
     Statistics 46
     Conclusions 50

4   **Managerial aspects** 52
     Who uses performance measures? 52
     How is performance measured? 54
     Points of inquiry 55
     Conclusions 67

5   **Conclusions** 69
     Constraints 69
     Politics 70
     Visibility and access 70
     The working environment 71

Appendix 74

Preface

Everywhere in the world a revolution is taking place, a transformation of business, and of the public services needed and wanted by people. At the heart of this revolution is management. There is a realization that, whatever the merits of how business and public services were organized and conducted in the past, new ways and new methods are essential for the future.

The background against which this revolution is taking place is one of economic, social and political turbulence and upheaval. The global environment is both unstable and volatile. The post-industrial economies of the West are undergoing radical transformation, driven by a combination of recession, technological advance and competition from emerging nations. This is compounded by the need for levels of investment and other resource commitments over periods of time that run contrary to prevailing political and economic pressures. The economies of the Far East have generated a business and commercial power bloc in the period since the Second World War that dominates the global electrical and consumer goods markets and makes them major operators in the car, white goods and finance sectors. This has been achieved through a combination of expertise, investment, technology and organization that emerged in the postwar reconstruction and regeneration.

Ever greater strains and demands are placed on the finite and diminishing resources of the world by an ever-increasing global population. These have to be arranged, planned, ordered and organized to ensure that they are used to greatest possible advantage. The combination of pressure on the one hand and finity on the other produce a drive for constant improvement in efficiency, effectiveness, maximization and optimization in all activities.

Never, therefore, has it been so essential to be able to measure accurately managerial and business performance. Organizations and managers who do this successfully are certain to give themselves advantages over those who do not, or those who simply pay lip service. The purpose of this report is to set the context for this; to explain and indicate the ways in which quantitative data is best used; to indicate and explain the ways in which qualitative aspects of organization and management are measured; and to set the whole against the complex and sophisticated background, an understanding of which is essential if performance is to be truly and accurately measured.

Richard Pettinger, September 1996

About the author

The author, Richard Pettinger, is an expert in human resource and industrial relations management. He has lectured, trained, consulted and advised extensively on all aspects of staff management and organizational behaviour.

He has advised on, prepared and presented industrial tribunal cases for both individuals and organizations. He has advised and consulted on the employment law aspects of privatization. He has advised, consulted and prepared procedures and standards of best practice and performance for private companies, public bodies, local authorities, national health trusts and not-for-profit organizations.

Richard Pettinger is the author of five other management books – *Introduction to Management* (Macmillan, 1994); *Preparing and Handling Industrial Tribunal Cases* (Technical Communications Ltd, 1995); *Introduction to Corporate Strategy* (Macmillan, 1996); *Introduction to Organizational Behaviour* (Macmillan, 1996); *Managing the Flexible Workforce* (Technical Communications Ltd, 1996) and *The Management of Discipline and Grievances* (STC Ltd, 1996).

The author is especially interested in working with all organizations wishing to raise their standards and understanding of staff management and industrial relations. He takes the view that excellent practice in these areas is a critical contribution to effective and profitable performance. He also consults and advises on all aspects of management practice, especially on the establishment of effective and positive standards of performance.

For further information, please contact:

Richard Pettinger
7 Victoria Place
Saltwood
Hythe
Kent CT21 4PY
Tel/Fax: (01303) 262388

1 Introduction

In general terms, all organizations in every sphere of activity are concerned with the same thing:

- maximizing customer, client and user satisfaction of their products and services over the long term;

- maximizing the confidence of everyone involved or affected by the organization over the long term;

- maximizing long-term owner/shareholder value, i.e. getting the best possible return on investment over the long term (and this applies to public services as well as commercial undertakings);

- securing the long-term future and well-being of the organization.

This all applies to private and commercial companies, public sector and service organizations, and the not-for-profit sector.

- For example, people buy cars from a garage on the basis that any faults can be put right in the future, and that the garage will maintain and service the car during the period of ownership. People buy groceries from a supermarket on the basis of its reputation for selling good food, and if for some reason an item is not good, it can be taken back and replaced. People would not buy from either the garage or the supermarket if they knew or perceived that neither would last long into the future, or if they had no general feeling of confidence in their ability to sustain themselves.

- The same applies to public services. People do not send their children to school where there is no confidence in the quality of education being offered. If it is announced that a school is to close, even if this is not to take place for a year or two, there is a rush to find alternatives with a more secure future. If there is no confidence that a hospital can treat a particular condition effectively, or if there is to be a long wait before it is able to do so, people will again seek alternatives – as demonstrated by the burgeoning UK private health-care sector.

- This is also found in the not-for-profit sector. People give to the causes represented by individual charities because they want their money to go to those whom it represents, or in whose interest it operates. They find other outlets for their giving if they have no confidence that particular charities have a future, or that their money is not being spent directly on the cause or client group. This is reflected in the ways in which the larger charities – Oxfam, NCH, NSPCC, RSPCA – have spent large amounts of resources on strengthening their institutions and identity (and not always to the satisfaction of long-term regular supporters). Nevertheless, they are securing their long-term existence in order to be able to operate more effectively in the future.

Prerequisites for Successful and Effective Performance

All of this is only achievable if some basic elements are present.

- *Clarity of purpose and direction:*

    – knowing where you are going and how to get there;

    – understanding the full implications and commitment necessary to achieve this.

- *Adequate levels of resources:* investment; information; technology; staff capability and expertise.

- *Knowledge and understanding:*

    – of the markets in which activities and operations are to take place and what customers and clients want and expect from them;

    – of what the organization's total capacity is, what it can and cannot achieve, and any operational implications arising;

    – of the total environment in which activities are to take place.

This gives the broad context in which performance is measured. It cannot be measured effectively if this is not fully understood.

Components of Successful Performance

Organizational and managerial performance is measured in the following areas.

- *Market standing:* overall organizational reputation; reputation of products and services; reputation of staff and their expertise; size of market served; location of market served; specific needs, wants and demands.

- *Market position:* actual market position in relation to desired position; the costs and benefits of maintaining this; opportunity costs; returns on resources; returns on investment.

- *Innovation:* capacity for innovation; desired and actual levels of innovation; time taken for new products and ideas to reach the market; attitudes to innovation; percentages of new products and ideas that become commercial successes.

- *Creativity:* expertise of staff; versatility and ability to diversify; capability for turning ideas into commercial successes; new product/service strike rates; attitudes to creativity; other related qualities, above all flexibility and responsiveness.

- *Resource utilization:* efficiency and effectiveness; balance of resources used in primary and support functions; wastage rates; resource utilization and added value.

- *Managerial performance:* total managerial performance; performance by function, department, division, group; performance at different levels of management – director, general manager, senior, middle, junior, supervisory, first-line.

- *Management development:* areas of strength and weakness; progress and improvement; desired expertise and capability; actual expertise and capability; development of specific skills and knowledge; desired and actual attitudes and behaviour; priority of training and development.

- *Staff performance:* areas of strength and weakness; progress and improvement; desired expertise and capability; actual expertise and capability; development of specific skills and knowledge; desired and actual attitudes and behaviour; attention to work patterns; commitment; extent and priority of training and development; targeting of training and development; attitudes to staff suggestions; specific positive and negative features.

- *Workforce structure:* core and peripheral; flexibility in attitudes and behaviour; multi-skilling; work patterns; general employability; continued future employability; relations between organization and workforce; relations between managers and staff; length and strength of hierarchies.

- *Wage and pay levels:* relationships between pay and output; relationships between pay, profits and performance; local factors and conditions; industrial factors and conditions; relationships between pay and expertise.

- *Organizational culture:* the extent to which this is positive/negative; identifying and removing negative factors; accentuating the positive; motivation and morale; staff policies; industrial relations; staff management.

- *Key relationships:* with backers; with staff; with suppliers; with distributors; with customers.

- *Public standing:* the respect and esteem in which the organization is held in its markets, the community, among its staff, customers and suppliers; confidence and expectations; general public factor coverage.

- *Profitability:* levels of profits accrued; timescales; means of measuring and assessing products; scope for enhancement and improvement.

- *Other factors:* general efficiency and effectiveness; product and service quality and value; areas for improvement; areas where complaints come from; opportunities and threats.

Many of these areas overlap. In some cases the same phrases are used under different headings and, without doubt, different words and phrases could be used to convey the same meanings. The mix and balance varies between organizations. However, every element is present in all situations to a greater or lesser extent. Initial lessons can therefore be drawn.

1. There is no single effective measure of performance in any situation or organization. Even if a supervisor is working to a single daily production target, he/she must have the right staff, adequately trained and motivated, the right volume and quality of components, and somewhere to put the finished items. And given the normal nature of work – all work – all this has to be available on a steady and continuous basis.

2.   A large proportion of the elements indicated are qualitative, not quantitative. The main qualities necessary to evaluate such factors properly are therefore judgment and analysis. Success and failure are value judgments placed on events and activities based on high levels of knowledge and expertise. Seldom, if ever, is success or failure self-evident except in the immediate or very short-term situation.

3.   It follows, in turn, that the main attributes of those who measure business and managerial performance have knowledge, expertise and understanding: of results; of the environment; of people; of customers and the market; of the product/services offered; of the organization's general position.

Information

None of this is possible without full, or at least adequate, information covering each of these areas and this must be constantly gathered and evaluated. Markets, technology, expertise are all constantly changing and organizations that do not respond have, at the very least, to recognize the effects that such a lack of response will, or may, have.

Full information enables organizations and their managers to reduce uncertainty, analyse levels of risk, maximize chances of success, minimize chances of failure and assess the prospects and likely consequences and outcomes of following particular courses of activity. It enables projections to be made for the organization as a whole and for each of its activities. Summary positions are often established under the headings of **strengths, weaknesses, opportunities, threats (SWOT)**, and these are most effective when related to the organization as a whole, to its markets, to its backers and stakeholders, and to its competitors.

Effective planning is also based on full information. The value of planning is at its greatest when it allows organizations:

*   to see the future as it unfolds, recognizing possible, likely and (more or less) certain developments;

*   to assess the continued performance of all activities and operations;

*   to assess the ways in which other people and organizations, especially competitors, are operating.

Effective planning is a process, the purpose of which is to arrive at and retain continued clarity of direction. It involves the analysis of the information; thinking it through, testing ideas; examining what is possible and what is not.

More specific schedules, practices, operations, activities, aims and objectives all then come from this body of knowledge and the understanding which arises from analysing it. Implementation and execution are then handed on to different people, functions, divisions and departments within the organization.

Note

It should be apparent from this that there is a world of difference between planning and plans. Dwight D. Eisenhower, the United States General and President, once said: *'Planning is everything, the plan is nothing.'* At their best, corporate and organizational plans are statements of what is now proposed as the result of information available, and are subject to change, modification and, when necessary, abandonment as and when circumstances change.

At their worst, they are detailed statements covering the way that the world is certain to be extending into the far distant future. No such position is sustainable now – indeed, it probably never was in the past. This does not prevent large corporations, both public and private, and the policy units of public services drawing these up. At best, they are an irrelevance. More usually, they constitute a waste of organizational resources that would be better used elsewhere. At worst, they are indeed slavishly followed in the teeth of a changing world and competitive environment with immense adverse consequences for the organization.

Responsibilities

Organizational Responsibilities

Specific organizational responsibilities exist in the following areas.

•   Anticipating the future in terms of the changing environment; anticipating changes in customer demands and perceptions; recognizing changes in the nature of competition; recognizing

changes in production and service technology; recognizing and anticipating changes in the nature of people attracted to work for the organization and the sector; recognizing and anticipating changes in the customer base.

- Investment as a continued commitment: in the areas of product development; quality improvement; management and staff training and development; production and service technology; the well-being of the customer.

- Organization development: in terms of its skills, knowledge, capabilities, attitudes and expertise; in terms of customer awareness and satisfaction; in terms of processes and procedures; in terms of supplier and distributor relations; in terms of its culture and structures.

- Training and development: of both management and staff in the skills, qualities, attributes and expertise necessary to secure the future; and in the key attitudes of flexibility, dynamism, responsiveness, willingness and commitment.

- Recognition of the fact that all organizations currently operate in a changing and turbulent environment; that historic and current success, efficiency, effectiveness and profitability is no guarantee that this will extend into the future. From this comes an obligation to ensure that all staff are capable of existing in this environment and that they are equipped with the resources and capability to do so.

- Openness: people respond to uncertainty and turbulence much better if they understand its extent and why they must constantly, update and develop. Organizations, therefore, have a clear duty to inform, consult and provide detail on all aspects of performance in general; and in more detail, concerning things which directly affect specific members and groups of staff.

- Ethics: long-term existence, the ability to secure the employment of staff, and establishing a regular and profitable customer base are enhanced by taking, accepting and understanding a view of the world as it really is. There is, therefore, a moral, as well as commercial, commitment.

Managerial Responsibilities

Specific managerial responsibilities exist in the following areas.

- To develop (and be developed in) capabilities and expertise required by the organization; required by the nature of professional management as it develops; and which involvement in the particular business, industry or service requires.

- To take a personal commitment to organizational success as well as that of the department, division or function for which the individual is responsible. High levels of personal commitment are required of all professions and professionals, in all spheres of activity and expertise, and this is also true of management and managers.

- To develop the full range of managerial skills and qualities required by the profession of management. This currently means being able to solve problems; manage people; set standards of performance; understand where the manager's domain fits into the wider scheme of things and total organizational performance; use resources efficiently and effectively; set and assess budgets; recognize the constraints under which operations have to be carried out; and generate a positive, open and harmonious culture and attitudes.

> At the heart of all organizational and managerial responsibility is the need to produce goods and services in the required volume and quality, at the right price, in the right place. This can only be achieved through having top-quality, expert and highly motivated staff. This is the critical factor in which the long-term future of the organization is secured and all effective measures of organization and managerial performance have this at their core.

Wider Considerations

Both organizations and their managers have to recognize that their performance is going to be measured and assessed by a variety of different people and in a great range of different ways. Everyone who comes into contact with an organization assesses it in one way or another. They may be summarized as follows.

- *The staff:* everyone who works for, and in, the organization and who is therefore dependent upon it for their income and spending power; this also applies to subcontractors and other retainers and potential staff.

- *The customers:* for continued satisfaction and service.

- *The communities:* in which staff and customers live and work, and in which the organization operates.

- *Social customers:* for example, charities, schools and hospitals which may approach the organization for sponsorship and support.

- *Backers:* shareholders, contributors, bankers, loan makers, venture capitalists, sponsors, city institutions, stock markets and public funds.

- *Suppliers of components and raw materials:* who have a vested interest in the success of the organization in terms of their own continuity of activity and profitability.

- *The community sectors and markets:* in which the organization offers its products and services for sale and consumption.

- *Distributors:* relying on their own position between the organization in question and the end users of the products or services for their continued existence.

- *Trade unions, market and employers' federations and associations:* that are active in the particular field.

- *Competitors and offerers of alternative products and services:* as part of their own quest for knowledge and expertise in the given field.

- *Lobbyists and vested interest groups:* related to the location of activities, the nature of activities and the ways in which those activities are carried out.

What Is Measured?

Performance is measured by each of these groups according to their own particular interest. For example, brilliant commercial performance may be rated very highly by consumers, but not by shareholders if this brilliant performance does not result in a rise in the share price.

When Is Performance Measured?

Managerial and business performance is measured continuously by each of the groups indicated. It is punctuated by formal and semi-formal events: annual reports; interim reports; staff performance appraisals; production and sales figures; pay rises and pay rounds; activity levels; budget efficiency and effectiveness.

These factors are dealt with extensively in Chapters 2, 3 and 4.

Aims and Objectives

All performance has to be measured against something and this is the reason for setting aims and objectives. Aims and objectives occur at different levels.

- *Corporate:* reflecting the overall scope of the organization; how it is to be run in structural and financial terms; how resources are to be allocated.

- *Competitive/business level:* how the organization is to compete in its different markets; which products and services should be developed and offered; the extent to which these meet customer needs; monitoring of product performance.

- *Operational:* how different functions of the organization contribute to total organizational purpose and activities.

- *Behavioural:* related to the human interactions between different parts of the organization; and between the organization, its customers and the wider community.

- *Confidence:* the generation of confidence and reputation among all those with whom it comes into contact.

- *Ethical:* meeting specific standards that may be enshrined in policy; the ability to work in certain activities, in certain locations; the attitude taken towards staff, customers and others with whom the organization comes into contact.

Aims and objectives should be SMART, that is:

- *Specific:* dealing with easily identifiable and quantifiable aspects of performance;

- *Measurable:* devised in ways so that success and failure can be identified;

- *Achievable:* striking a balance between maximizing/optimizing resources and output without setting standards so high that targets are unattainable and therefore unvalued;

- *Recognizable:* understood by all concerned;

- *Time constrained:* so that a continuous record of progress and achievement may be kept and problem areas identified.

Whatever is determined has therefore to be capable of:

- reconciling these differing and often conflicting pressures;

- attending to all aspects of organizational performance;

- providing distinctive measures of success and failure;

- enhancing the total performance of the organization;

- where necessary, reconciling the different and conflicting demands of particular stakeholders and interested parties.

No single set of generic objectives exists. All aims and objectives must be drawn up against the organization's specific context and background if they are to have any meaning. Whatever they refer to, they must reflect the following questions.

- What contribution does this activity/set of activities make to total organizational performance? Where does this fit into the broader objectives of the department, division or function concerned? Where does this fit into the wider purpose of the organization?

- What resources, equipment, information, technology and expertise are needed to carry it out successfully?

- What specific restraints are there – for example: can it be done straight away? Are there other things that must first be done? How long does it/will it/must it take?

Aims and objectives therefore attend to both the broad and the precise, and must be set in the context of organizational activity.

Organizational Activity

Levels of Activity

Two main levels of activity are distinguished:

- *steady-state:* conducting and organizing activities in regularized ways;

- *crisis:* anticipating and handling problems and unexpected incidents.

Other levels may also be identified:

- *pioneering:* innovation, creativity, invention and development;

- *policy:* setting standards of behaviour and performance;

- *maintenance and improvement:* of HR, technology, communications, administration and systems, production, marketing, sales.

Levels of Performance

Traditionally three levels of performance are distinguished:

- *unsatisfactory:* remedied as and when it happened;

- *excellent:* high levels of output, quality and satisfaction, achieved by very few, mostly leaders in particular fields;

- *satisfactory:* achieved (or assumed to be achieved) by most organisations over long periods, reflected in adequate levels of profit, success and effectiveness (and often not measured any more deeply).

The present drive is away from satisfactory towards constant improvement and excellence.

Core and Peripheral Activities

- *Core activities* are those which bring in the main level of income; constitute the primary area of activity; give the organization its main image and identity.

- *Peripheral activities* are those profitably engaged in as the result of additional capacity; easy access to markets; additional use of technology.

Conclusions

The purpose of this introductory chapter is to set the context for measuring all aspects of organizational and managerial performance and to introduce the means by which this is to be done. It is not possible to do this effectively or successfully in isolation – and the fact that some organizations nevertheless attempt this does not make it right. Without this basis, both quantitative and qualitative performance measures have no meaning to those who are allocated more specific performance targets. Lack of any context is also one of the main reasons why performance appraisal schemes directed at human resources fall into disrepute. Whatever is done must be understood and acceptable to those involved. Acceptability springs from understanding and this is based, in turn, on the effective communication of the right and required information to those involved. This applies to everything except cases of unethical or criminal activities.

This approach to knowing and understanding the broader context enables specific problems and blockages to be identified early. These may be operational, behavioural, procedural or political. Each becomes more likely, the larger and more sophisticated the organization and its managerial and administrative systems.

Finally, the greater the understanding of this background and context, the greater the level of true assessment of organization capacity and potential. Total performance can then be measured against this, and department, division or functional group and individual aims and objectives may be set much more precisely.

2 Qualitative measures of performance

Introduction

Business and managerial performance measurement is largely qualitative. This is because organizations are created and staffed by people, and because their customers, clients and users are people also. Moreover, the most overtly mathematical and precise measures of performance have to be seen in the context in which they are established and then judged and evaluated by those responsible.

For example, a 35% increase in sales is an overtly easy and straightforward measure. However, the following elements have still to be addressed:

- the time period over which the increase is to take place;

- whether the 35% increase is required across the board, or whether an overall increase of 35% will do;

- whether the 35% would be covered by a one-off purchase or windfall;

- whether, if the 35% increase is fulfilled the following week, the target will be revised for the future;

- whether this is a reflection of the capacity and capability of the rest of the organization;

- whether this is within the workforce's capability, whether overtime will have to be worked, or whether new staff will have to be taken on;

- any questions of location – are there any questions of specific market/localized constraints; the extent to which it is related to relative levels of prosperity in the market;

- the wider state of the market; the activities of competitors; whether the market is capable of sustaining this (or any other level of increase);

- whether the 35% increase represents an increase in the total market, or whether it means taking market share from competitors;

- and finally, where does the figure of 35% come from, who decided it, and on what grounds?

Once this form of judgment and evaluation has been made, the behaviour of customers, consumers and clients has to be considered. For example, the buyer may come into the establishment, not receive instant service, and turn round or storm out. Or a salesperson may be so busy giving excellent satisfaction to one customer that the next customer is delayed, leading to dissatisfaction on their part. Or they may be dealt with by a good salesperson who has nothing to offer to the customer; or by a bad salesperson, who nevertheless persuades the customer to buy, leading to an instant sale but subsequent dissatisfaction.

The process cannot therefore possibly be completely objective or rational. Qualifying performance effectiveness and success therefore relies on:

- recognizing the human signs of buyer behaviour and attitudes;

- recognizing the human signs of organizational behaviour and attitudes;

- recognizing the convergence and divergence of priorities and objectives;

- recognizing the importance and influence of stakeholders and participants.

The best approach is to identify the most likely outcome in the most sets of circumstances, to concentrate primarily on this, and to deal with exceptions as and when they arise.

Priorities

Ideally, priorities are established to ensure concentration of organizational resources to best commercial or service advantage in the pursuit of long-term customer, client and user satisfaction. In practice, it is rarely possible to achieve everything desired or required. Two basic approaches are possible, as illustrated in Figure 2.1.

There is nothing intrinsically right or wrong with either approach indicated in Figure 2.1. The main issue at the outset is to know which approach is being taken and the opportunities and consequences of that choice.

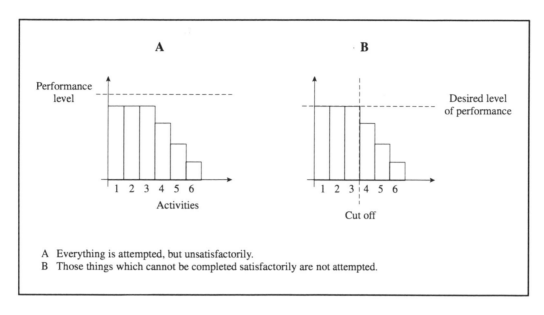

Figure 2.1 Establishing priorities.

Objectives

Objectives are:

- *organizational:* reflecting the overall purpose and direction;

- *departmental/divisional/functional:* reflecting the contribution that each is expected to make to the whole;

- *managerial:* reflecting the contribution that different managers are expected/anticipated to make to the overall direction;

- *professional/occupational:* reflecting the need for professional and occupational satisfaction in different staff and work categories;

- *personal:* reflecting more general needs, especially those of job security, enhanced reward and prosperity, and advancement.

Convergence and Divergence of Objectives

It is essential to recognize the existence of these differing objectives. The best and most successful and effective organizations harmonize personal, professional and occupational objectives with those of the organization as a whole. Where this is not possible, á certain amount of dysfunction/malfunction occurs.

For example, a manager charged with responsibility for introducing a new education policy knows that this will take several years to evaluate for success. The manager's political masters want tangible results within three months. The next promotion in the manager's career is dependent upon the satisfaction of the political masters with their performance. The manager has therefore to reconcile the following:

- delivering the initiative professionally;

- advancing their own career;

- doing the work to the satisfaction of the political masters.

It is clear that doing the job properly requires persuading the political masters that a three-month measure is neither feasible nor legitimate in the circumstances. It is also clear that, on the face of it, there exists a real discrepancy between doing the job properly and receiving personal reward, recognition and advancement.

The greatest success is achieved where the potential problems have been recognized and steps have been taken to harmonize and integrate these different forms of objectives.

Failure is likely where no/little recognition exists of the problem. Where it is not possible to integrate organizational and personal/professional objectives, recognition of the effects on performance (especially long-term performance) is essential. Problem areas for the future can then at least be more clearly identified.

Moreover, levels of motivation and morale are normally much higher where objectives in each category are harmonized. Where objectives do diverge and conflict, people always pursue their personal and professional objectives rather than those of the organization.

Motivation

Highly motivated and committed staff produce high quality work over long periods of time. The highest levels of motivation occur in organizations which:

- respect and value their staff as people; treat them equally; offer opportunities on an even and equal basis; concentrate on performance not personality; and pay and reward their people well;

- generate positive and harmonious culture; take early action to remove negative attitudes where they start to emerge; reward contributions to organizational performance;

- recognize that everyone has personal, professional and occupational drives, aims and objectives that require satisfaction; and take steps to harmonize and integrate these with organizational purposes;

- balance the key behavioural features of expectation, effort and reward;

- recognize and reward achievement, development and progress;

- balance the attention given to the work in hand, the workings of work groups and individual performance;

- recognize the prevalence and influence of those elements that, if right, tend to motivate; and those that, if wrong, tend to demotivate.

Demotivators	Motivators
• Management/supervisory style	• Value
• Administrative overload	• Respect
• Length of chains of command	• Esteem
• Attention to procedures rather than output	• Responsibility
• Bad communications	• Progress
• Lack of respect/value/esteem	• Achievement
• Status/importance based on rank rather than achievement	• Communications

The fundamental concern is to have capable people on the staff who want to work. The best and most rewarding jobs in the world can be – and are – destroyed by negative styles and attitudes of management. The most overtly mundane jobs in the world can be – and are – transformed and made excellent by positive and supportive styles of management and by offering respect, value and recognition where it is possible.

High Levels of Motivation

High levels of motivation are indicated by:

- low levels of absenteeism;

- low levels of turnover;

- low levels of accidents, sickness and injury;

- few disputes, personality clashes, inter-departmental wrangles;

- open approach to problems; early recognition and attention to potential problems;

- active participation in consultation, organizational initiatives, suggestion schemes.

In each case, these are reinforced by open and participative styles of management; ready access to organizational, functional and personal information; and clear and simple systems and procedures.

Low Levels of Motivation

These are indicated by:

- high/increasing levels of disputes and grievances; high/increasing levels of disciplinary cases and the use of disciplinary procedures;

- high/increasing levels of accidents, sickness and injury;

- high/increasing levels of absenteeism and turnover;

- steady decline in quality and quantity of performance over the medium to long term. This is reinforced by the concentration of attention on procedures and systems rather than output, and by the proliferation of new systems, procedures and monitoring and support functions.

These are the initial indicators of high and low levels of motivation. The key areas to address when assessing levels of staff motivation and morale are:

- the level and nature of identity that the staff have with the organization; the extent to which status, esteem and rewards are issued for productive output as distinct from adherence to procedures;

- the ability to offer fulfilment, recognition accomplishment to all levels and grades of staff.

Everyone has basic needs for a sense of belonging, self-respect and self-worth, the respect and value of others, and the need for growth, development and progress. Initial enquiries in this area are, therefore, to be made along these lines, and these are the key features to address where problems are found to exist.

Induction

The purpose of induction is to get all members of staff as productive as possible, as quickly as possible. To do this, organizations attend to matching their own needs with those of individuals, and to ensuring that what is required of them is stated as clearly as possible at the outset. If this is to be effective, the following matters have to be addressed:

- setting the attitudes and standards of behaviour required, ensuring that new employees know what is expected of them and that they conform to expectations and requirements; that they understand the ways in which they are to work, as well as what they have to do;

- job training and familiarization, concerned with matching individual expertise to the ways of working required by the organization;

- introductions to new work colleagues and key contacts as part of the process of gaining confidence, understanding and mutuality of objectives that is essential for the development of effective and successful working relationships and job performance;

- familiarization with the environment, premises, ways of working and particular obligations on the part of the employer; and ensuring that the new employee understands his/her position in the organization and environment.

Organizations that do this successfully go to much trouble to ensure that this is adequately and effectively completed. They recognize the returns on an excellent and well-resourced induction process in the production of highly motivated, clearly focused and committed workforces.

It is also essential to recognize that induction is started in general terms by any vague impression that the new employee has picked up of the organization. It will have further been reinforced if, for example, he/she has been a customer or client of it in the past. Any correction of these impressions must be addressed as part of the induction process which will also be reinforced by the way in which selection and assessment is carried out.

Performance Appraisal

The purpose of performance appraisal is to measure the performance of individuals and/or groups at the place of work. Performance appraisal of the human resource also reflects the standard and quality of activity in each functional and occupational division and category. For performance appraisal to be effective and successful, the following elements must be present.

- Preset, pre-agreed aims and objectives, clearly understood by all concerned. These should be prioritized with deadlines for achievement. Performance targets should be realistic and achievable, balancing the need for effective and improved performance against effective resource utilization. If targets are unrealistic they will be ignored; if they are too easy they set a wider agenda for the lowering of performance standards.

- Appraisal is a process which consists of a series of regularized formal reviews at which targets and objectives are discussed and assessed for success and failure. This forms a continuous relationship between appraiser and appraisee that both builds confidence and understanding, and also enables particular issues and problems to be identified early.

- Appraisal must be flexible and dynamic, and part of the wider process of ensuring that the organization's purpose is being adhered to.

- Appraisal is a participative process at its best between appraiser and appraisee, which again helps to ensure a mutual confidence and commitment.

- Appraisal must be believed in and valued by all concerned; it must be adequately resourced and prioritized.

- Appraisal must provide a basis for action, so that whatever is agreed during the process or at a formal review is acted upon by both appraiser and appraisee.

- Formal reviews should take place at least every three–six months; if they are more frequent than this, they tend to impose on the continuing process and relationship that should also be present; if they are less frequent, it becomes very difficult to conduct an adequate or genuine review of what has been done over the past period.

Particular performance appraisal schemes may seek to provide merit pay awards, identify potential, identify training and development needs, identify job–person match and mismatch, identify organization development needs, identify poor and substandard performance, check achievement against agreed objectives and agree individual objectives for the future.

Appraisal schemes fall into disrepute for the following reasons:

- they are neither believed in nor valued;

- they do not contribute to the wider success of the organization;

- are bureaucratic or mechanistic;

- it is the scheme and its paperwork that are important, and not the process;

- the reviews are too infrequent or missed altogether;

- and what is promised in them (e.g. pay awards, training, promotion, development) is not delivered in practice.

They also suffer from performance criteria being identified in general terms only. This leads to inconsistency in application, leading in turn, to unevenness and unfairness in the award of pay rises, places on training courses, opportunities and promotion.

The best performance appraisal schemes are completely open. They are conducted on the basis of mutual understanding, trust and honesty between appraiser and appraisee. If staff are asked to declare shortcomings in their recent performance and if this is then used as a stick with which to beat them, they will simply not do it.

It follows, therefore, that there is a necessary body of skills and knowledge required of managers in the conduct of effective performance appraisal. This has to be underpinned by the presence of positive attitudes and a determination to improve performance rather than find fault. Communication, articulation, target and objective setting, counselling, support, trust, dependency and assertiveness are all clearly necessary. If this

is the basis on which performance appraisal is conducted, there is plenty of scope for picking up genuine poor performance and dealing with frustrated and recalcitrant employees in particular situations.

The control of appraisal must always rest with the manager, and while agreement of objectives with a member of staff is desirable, this should never be at the expense of diluted or substandard performance.

Appraisers

Many people have a legitimate interest in the appraisal of staff and organizational performance. These are:

- *the immediate superior:* because they have the most detailed and up-to-date knowledge of what the appraisee has been doing;

- *the 'grandparent':* to take a wider view of the performance;

- *peers:* the great advantage of peer appraisal is that a person's colleagues have an excellent general appreciation of what is being carried out;

- *subordinates:* this is especially effective on questions of management staff, volume and quality of communication, and general management style;

- *self-appraisal:* which is most effective where complete openness, trust and honesty exist between appraiser and appraisee.

For appraisal to succeed and survive, it must reflect wider organizational values and may be used to symbolize, sustain and develop particular types of culture. Performance appraisal is at its worst where it simply resorts to unqualified checklists, or where there is a conspiracy that avoids genuine measurement of performance and individual contribution.

Occupational Health

Organizations are increasingly assuming responsibility for the good health of their staff and taking positive steps and making interventions that are designed to ensure this. Part of this consists of determining that the employee is fit and healthy when he/she first starts work and that this continues throughout the period of employment. Part of this also consists of ensuring a healthy and safe working environment – and taking the widest possible view of this, which

increasingly means providing good quality general facilities, designating the workplace as a no-smoking area, and providing regular general health checks for employees. Those who have persistent or regular time away from work may be required to have medical assessments by company medical staff as well as the employee's own doctor. It may also require employees to take medical treatment at the behest of the organization as a precondition of continuing to work for it. In the best cases, occupational health schemes are particularly strong and valuable in the diagnosis of job-specific illnesses and injuries. They also provide a general source of medical knowledge by which the organization may assess the overall state of their workforce's health and identify particular occupational problems.

Particular matters of current concern, and major issues of which managers and organizations should be aware, are:

- stress, its causes and effects; techniques for the management and limitation of stress;

- repetitive strain injuries (RSI), which are/can be caused by continuous use of certain muscles or the carrying out of certain activities – for example, continuous keyboard working;

- back injuries, caused either by bad lifting practices or continuous bad back posture (which again, may be caused by sitting in a single position for long periods of time);

- the effects of VDU screens on eye sight; the effects of sitting at a VDU for long periods on muscles; specific effects of VDU working on pregnant women;

- industrial and commercial heating and lighting and the relationship between these and eye strain, coughs, colds and other minor, but recurrent, ailments;

- smoking, both active and passive, and its effects on all staff (both in relation to general health and also concerns such as odours and environmental pleasantness);

- alcohol abuse;

- HIV and Aids, and the implications for particular workplaces and occupations, especially for those who come into contact with client groups and other members of the public.

All matters relating to occupational health are interrelated, and together constitute a greater attention to the needs of workplace human resource management. A positive approach to the maintenance of the human resource has also been demonstrated generally to have advantageous effects on morale and motivation, and reductions in accidents, sickness and absenteeism. Connections are also made between the adoption of a positive approach to human resource maintenance and attention to the areas indicated, and organization success, effectiveness and profitability.

The converse is also true – that alienation, demotivation and low morale are most prevalent where the human resource is not maintained. Priorities and initiatives in these areas therefore have a positive impact on the performance of the human resource, and therefore of the organization as a whole. Some of this has arisen as the result of increased general awareness; some of it has arisen also as the result of organizations assuming wider responsibilities for their people.

Pay, Remuneration and Reward

The purpose of a payment system is to:

- reward productive effort and output;

- provide an adequate level of income on a regular basis;

- motivate and encourage, and meet the expectations of those carrying out the work.

Those who devise payment systems have also to understand the wider motivations and expectations of job holders, and either meet these as far as possible, or else understand the consequences of not meeting them. In general terms, the factors necessary include:

- consistency, stability and security;

- a match between achievement and reward;

- compensation for loss of purchasing power due to inflation;

- the ability to share in the wider success of the organization.

This is reflected in organizational needs to attract, retain and reward high quality and expert staff. If this is to be successful, the expectations of those staff must be met. Anything that is proposed must therefore be based on an understanding of these expectations and those things that do actually attract, retain and reward.

Bad and unvalued payment systems cause instability and labour turnover of their own accord. The key consequence of a bad system is extreme demotivation and demoralization, and this in turn leads to declining and reduced levels of output, both quantity and quality. It is also necessary to recognize the inherent nature of the work. No amount of money will make a boring job interesting but merely more bearable. Similarly, it is possible to offer intrinsic benefits in inherently interesting or fulfilling jobs by paying attention to the other motivating factors where there may be constraints and reward packages based purely on salary.

indicators of motivation & good pay — labour turnover, etc...

Components of Wage, Salary and Reward Packages

There are five elements as follows.

- *Payments:* annual, quarterly, monthly, four-weekly, weekly, daily; commission, bonus, increments, fees; profit, performance and merit related payments.

- *Allowances:* attendance, disturbance, shift, weekend, unsocial hours, training and development, location and relocation, absence from home.

- *Benefits:* loans (e.g. for season tickets); pension (contributory or non-contributory); subsidies (on company products, canteen, travel); car; telephone/car phone; private health care; training and development; luncheon vouchers; help with school fees.

- *Chains of gold or super benefits:* school holidays (teachers); cheap loans (banks); free/cheap travel (railways, shipping, airlines); pension arrangements (for older or longer serving staff).

- *Other benefits:* occupational health; nurseries; specific healthcare options (e.g. medical, dental); life assurance; long-term healthcare and permanent health insurance schemes; flexitime; cash alternatives to all these options.

This is very complex and the mixes adopted by organizations when devising and implementing reward strategies cover a variety of particular aims and objectives in response to particular situations and in meeting the expectations of particular categories of staff.

Performance, Profit and Merit Payment Schemes

The basis of any such scheme must be to relate as precisely as possible the rewards to staff with the effectiveness and success of the work that they carry out and the outputs that they achieve. For such schemes to be effective, the following conditions must exist:

- schemes must be believed in, valued and understood by all concerned;

- targets must be achievable; they must be set in advance; and if they are achieved, payment must always be made;

- the language and presentation of the scheme should be positive and aimed at 'rewards for achievement'; the scheme's rules should not be couched in bureaucratic phraseology;

- performance-related pay is not a means of cutting wage and salary bills – any form of performance-related pay normally increases salary bills. If schemes are used with the covert purpose of reducing salary bills, this always leads to demotivation, demoralization and antagonism on the part of the staff;

- objectives, criteria and other measures of performance must be drawn in a way so that everybody understands them and they can be measured;

- it must serve the aspirations of all those categories of staff affected.

The best and most effective way of making performance- and profit-related payments is to reward everybody on an equal basis. The most equitable form is to allocate bonuses to people on an equal percentage of salary – so that, for example, in public services where a budget saving is made, everyone is rewarded by being given $x\%$ of salary; in private services where particular profit targets are achieved, again the bonus is an equal percentage on salary.

Ethics

There is a direct correlation between the taking of a strong moral and ethical stance and long-term profitability. Examples of this can be drawn from all over the world. The Japanese car and electrical goods companies set high standards of probity and integrity, and through their published documentation, place the onus on their managers to deliver. The Body Shop has made a strong and highly profitable feature of its concern for the

environment and the standards that it has set in its dealings with the Third World. MacDonald's have set absolute standards of quality, cleanliness, value and service across every operation, everywhere in the world.

These approaches can be broken down into the following components.

- Disclosure of information in terms of volume, quality and honesty.

- Employment issues, pay, benefits and conditions; industrial democracy; equality of opportunity; information, participation and consultation.

- The nature of community involvement and relations with the environment.

- The nature of political involvement and donations to political parties, candidates, vested interests and pressure groups; donations and support for charities and 'worthy causes'.

- The nature of products and services – with particular emphasis on contentious areas such as tobacco, alcohol, drugs, pharmaceuticals and military equipment.

- Marketing policies and attitudes to customers, consumers, client groups; the nature and quality of advertising.

- A general respect for people and life.

- The moral components of organizational strategy and purposes; categories of concern which may be divided into the *broad* – the world, the nation, the local community; and the *narrow* – industry, the organization, the sector.

- The range of concerns that *ought* to be considered by organizations.

- Public interest, public lobbies and pressure groups; specific interests including socio-political groups, lobbies and fringe interests.

- Ordinary common decency.

This is a highly qualitative and subjective checklist. However, organizations that enjoy high levels of esteem and respect always do so because their general conduct stands up to social and ethical scrutiny as well as commercial viability. It is very difficult to find examples where commercial

success has been achieved without consideration of social factors or public acceptance except in the very short term. In the longer term, organizations have to operate in, and be acceptable to, their staff, customers and communities. For this to occur, a positive, mutual and continuing respect is necessary. This is always damaged, and often destroyed, when the general integrity of particular organizations is called into question.

Organizations therefore have to have full knowledge and understanding of what is acceptable, both globally and locally. This extends to all spheres of business operation. Marketing initiatives strike a balance between being positive and exciting, while at the same time stopping well short of making claims for the product that are simply not true or presenting something in ways unacceptable to sectors of the communities. Successful staff management is based on mutual respect and trust, as well as effective work organization. General management is always more successful where those involved understand why they are doing things in particular ways and can trust the organization to lead them successfully and effectively in the proposed directions, and then deliver the desired results. The production of shoddy or inadequate goods is only feasible until another organization comes along with improved, adequate and satisfactory products with which to replace them.

Administration

Administration exists to support primary functions. Administrative functions create and operate procedures that are used to:

* control expenditure;

* provide information;

* attend to the human side of enterprise;

* monitor progress;

* resolve problems.

Measuring the performance of support functions and administration refers first and foremost to the contribution that they make to primary activities. To preach perfection, no other position is sustainable. Any system or procedure that hinders or dilutes primary performance is to be abolished and replaced, or reformed.

The best procedures and systems are simple and clear to understand by everyone concerned. They attend to:

- *finance:* providing clear and adequate information as to what organizational resources are being used so that judgments may be made as to their effectiveness;

- *human resource management procedures and functions:* in the areas of discipline and grievance handling; health and safety at work; consultation and participation; negotiation (where collective bargaining still exists); and procedures with a quick and effective resolution of problems and disputes;

- *progress chasing and quantity assurance:* so that blockages, shortcomings and shortfalls can be identified early and addressed successfully; so that customer orders can be prioritized and reconciled;

- *quality assurance:* picking up customer complaints early and resolving them quickly.

The main problems with administrative systems and procedures arise when they become too complex to be handled quickly and effectively. This leads to teams of staff being taken on in support functions which have then to be sustained by the primary activities. This is true for both public services and private sector activities. Any extensive recruitment and development of support functions is to be seen in this context. Again, no other position is sustainable.

Problems also arise when head offices of giant and complex corporations, public services and multinational companies ask for performance targets, especially revenue targets, because of the cost of their own sustenance and maintenance.

More specifically, they arise in public services when cuts in primary services are made to accommodate requested expenditure on support functions.

Conclusions

Qualitative measurement of performance is dependent upon the expertise, knowledge and understanding of those who measure it. It depends for success on knowing and understanding each of the elements indicated above. Each element – objectives, motivation, appraisal, payment and ethics or absolute standards – have to be reconciled with each other, and then in turn reconciled with:

- the level of service that customers, clients and users desire;

- the organizational form, structure, skills, knowledge and attitudes required to do this;

- the collective and individual values, attitudes and behaviour required;

- a detailed understanding and acceptance of the required nature of performance;

- commitment to remedy failure, build on success and continuously improve.

Attention to these aspects is the key to sustained high levels of performance. Except in the very short term, high levels of high-quality output are not possible where morale is low, where staff are unvalued and under-rewarded, where standards of probity and honesty do not exist and where performance in all areas is not measured and appraised as effectively as possible. Even in a wider environment, where there are ostensibly too many people chasing too few jobs and too little work, those organizations that maximize their performance in the long term concentrate their efforts on performance measurement in the ways indicated in this chapter. This is also the key to selecting the correct quantitative aspects, as well as being the basis for their judgment and evaluation.

3 Quantitative aspects of performance

Introduction

All organizations should – and do – produce amounts of mathematical, statistical and financial information about themselves, their markets, their competitors, their suppliers, their customers and their staff. This is essential. It is not, however, an end in itself. How this information is used, who uses it and for what reasons are of equal importance. The need to understand what the figures and numbers indicate is therefore vital and this varies between the different interested parties.

Top managers and directors use this information to assess the continued success of the current and envisaged direction of the organization. They draw this from output and sales figures, financial returns and the total financial position indicated.

Departmental, divisional and functional directors and managers receive information specific to their particular areas and use this to assess the success and value of their own contribution to the organization as a whole.

Increasingly, all staff have access to information on organizational performance. It is a vital and legitimate interest to them after all – business and financial strength means continuity of work and employment, while weakness calls this into question.

Customers use the information as part of their requirement for having their expectations met, maintaining confidence and having access to products and services in the future.

Auditors have to sign annual (and increasingly interim) financial figures as being a true and fair representation of the financial size of the organization, its scale of operations and the sources of the funding on which it is based.

Stock market analysts use the information to predict the future performance of the shares of public companies. They also use this information to decide whether or not to invest their own and clients' funds in one organization in preference to others.

Bankers, venture capitalists and other actual and potential backers use the figures as the basis for deciding whether to invest in a particular company, project, product or product range in preference to others, and for the general soundness and viability of these activities.

All figures are therefore subject to a variety of uses and interpretations. Each of the groups indicated has its own particular brief to which to work. This is the context in which quantitative measurement of organizational and management performance is to be seen.

Finance

All organizations are ultimately judged on the strength of their financial performance. To do this successfully, it is necessary to address:

- costs;

- financial structure;

- sectoral economics and returns;

- projections and forecasts;

- level of dividends.

Costs

The following costs must be distinguished.

- *Fixed costs (FC):* these are the costs incurred by all organizations, whether or not any profitable or effective business of any sort is conducted. They consist of capital charges, premises costs, staff costs and administrative, managerial and support function overheads.

- *Variable costs (VC):* these are the costs incurred as the result of engaging in direct activities. They consist of raw materials, packaging and distribution costs. The amount of each varies according to the levels of activity.

- *Marginal costs (MC):* this is the cost incurred by the production of one extra item of output. This reflects the extent to which the production capacity of the organization may be extended without incurring additional fixed costs in the form of investment in new plant, staff, equipment or machinery. There comes a point at which the production of an extra item pushes the organization to its total current capacity, and when the production of one more item requires this additional level of investment.

- *Opportunity costs (OC):* this is what is forgone as the result of engaging in a given set of activities – by doing one thing, an organization is not able to do other things.

- *Coercive costs (CC):* these occur when the nature of activities or the state of the market make it impossible or very difficult *not* to pursue a particular line. For example, it may be 'essential' for a retail chain to establish a presence in an expensive shopping mall rather than (or as well as) continuing its high street operations because with whom it competes are doing so, and because therefore the customer base is concentrated in the mall.

Prices and Charges

Price and charge levels normally cover variable costs and marginal costs, and also make a contribution to fixed costs. This is not as simple as it sounds, however:

- people are attracted by the range and quality of an organization's offerings;

- people buy what they need, want and can afford.

The two are not always the same. It is necessary, therefore, to assess products and services as:

- those which attract;

- those which sell;

- those which make money.

Part of the fixed cost – the overall obligation – is to cover each element. This means carrying those products which attract in order to be able to sell those that sell and those that make money. Reductions in the total range – especially those that attract – may cause erstwhile customers to look elsewhere for satisfaction.

Product clusters have also to be recognized. For example, a shop that sells razor blades may do so at a loss (i.e. less than variable cost); however, it more than covers this through its sales of razors and shaving cream. Customers are effectively buying a shave. If the razor blades are withdrawn, customers may look elsewhere to buy their shave.

Variable costs may also not be covered:

- when loss leaders are used to attract customers to the organization. Again, the aim is to recoup losses in the long term with surpluses from the sales of other goods;

- in the short to medium term, when an organization is investing heavily in some longer-term objective, e.g. brand strengthening. Or it may be that a product can be marked right down because after-sales or product insurance can be marked up and the variable cost more than recouped.

Cost Apportionment

Cost apportionment can be used to allocate the proportion of fixed cost/total cost to each product or service unit. Its great weakness is that it puts artificial constraints on the ability to price individual items at commercial levels.

Cost apportionment is best used in the measurement and allocation of variable costs because it reinforces the accuracy. This is a much more flexible and accurate guide of the true cost of getting products through production processes to market.

Rather than apportioning fixed costs, it is best to recognize that the main costs that an organization carries are fixed, a consequence of being in that line of activity. Fixed costs are best covered by ensuring that each sale or cluster of sales makes a contribution to the fixed costs; this is certain to occur provided that it more than covers the variable cost. From this, it is possible to work out the number of sales necessary to remain viable over given periods of time and this can be related to forecasts, projections and market analyses.

Financial Structure

The basic financial size and strength – and therefore structure – arises from:

- *companies:* sales of shares; loans; mortgages; debentures; venture capital; private backing; and income from sales;

- *government departments:* allocation of funds and budgets; (increasingly) sale of services, either on nominal or full cost basis;

- *not-for-profit:* income from contributors and supporters; grants and donations.

This represents the *investment* made by the particular backers. In each case a positive return is sought – profits and dividends from companies; effective and efficient public services from government; improvements in the position of the client groups of charities.

Size

The effectiveness of financial size is determined by its overall purpose, the ability to raise finance from its different sources and the size of the market or client group that it seeks to serve. This is then related to its stated aims, objectives and purposes. Assessment can then be made as to whether or not it can meet them all; and if not, whether it takes the decision to attempt everything or to drop some activities.

Strength

Financial strength is assessed on the ability of the organization to survive in its field over the long term.

Gearing

The basic strength of companies is determined by the proportion of share capital and retained profits to other forms of backing, especially loans. The higher the proportion of loans, the higher and more disadvantageous the gearing.

General instability is higher also. Loan-makers may seek repayments at the end of the loan period. If they do not renew the loan, the organization is left with a financial hole to fill.

Loan interest also adds to fixed costs and total costs; where this is a high proportion of total financial strength, it represents a serious charge on the business.

Public Finance

The financial strength of public services is determined by the extent and willingness of central and local government bodies and departments to support them. Public finance is also heavily based on percentage variances on the amount allocated to particular functions during the previous year or period. This assumes that:

- the amount allocated for the previous period was more or less adequate;

- the amount allocated for the previous period was capable of sustaining adequate and effective public services;

- the percentage variation, whether up or down, will be adequate for the coming period.

Not-for-Profit

The financial strength of not-for-profit organizations is determined by their continued ability to attract donors, sponsorship, support and grants to be used in the service of their client groups.

This is called a variable income base. It changes according to general levels of prosperity of the society in which the donors live. It is also affected by movements in perceptions of the client groups, whether upwards or downwards – enhanced or more positive perceptions lead to increased income and vice versa. The ability to generate income is also affected by the introduction of more pressing concerns. The specific problem is to sustain a strong and stable organization, and meet its fixed costs without being able to draw either on shareholders' funds or government finance.

Sectoral Economics

All activities have their own 'brand of economics'. This means they have their own mix of activity volumes, patterns of investment, fixed and variable costs, pricing and charging capability and policies, and desired, anticipated and possible returns. For example:

- Construction economics requires the companies involved to have the capability to finance projects from inception through development and agreement, and through the duration of the project to satisfactory delivery; to acquire specialist equipment and staff as and when necessary; to finance steady-state activities over a period of months and, in the case of large projects, many years.

- Health economics requires organizations to have the capability to fund health care and development over indeterminate periods of time; to acquire specialist equipment; to acquire products of

medical research – drugs, treatments – as and when necessary or desired; to contribute to health research and advancement.

- Corner shop economics requires the ability to satisfy large volumes of small purchase customers; to acquire and present a range of products to sustain this; to generate sufficient cashflow in the short term to enable stocks to be replenished.

Financial strength is therefore further assessed by relating the features of the particular backgrounds and sectors to those organizations that wish to operate in them, and by recognizing the opportunities and constraints present.

Projections and Forecasts

Financial projections and forecasts are carried out on the basis of analysing the information available and relating it to informed assumptions about the levels of activity. They are used to predict the possible and likely outcomes of future activities.

They evaluate alternatives and measure the likely success, failure, profitability and risk of particular courses of action.

They provide informed bases for the analysis of future product and market performance.

They provide information on the useful life of organization technology, skills and expertise.

They identify the best, medium and worst outcomes in each of these areas and pinpoint inherent risks and rewards available.

They identify returns on activities in terms of:

- simple payback – how quickly will the initial investment be repaid?

- average rate of return – what is the daily/weekly/monthly/ quarterly/annual average for a longer-term initiative?

- specific volumes of activity at given prices, and the effects of price variances on desired and required levels of activity and projections of income.

Dividends

Dividends are the rewards available to investors. These fall into the following categories.

- *Financial:* payments made by organizations to shareholders and other backers in return for their investment and loyalty.

- *Goods and services:* provision of these at advantageous rates to backers and shareholders.

- *Political:* positive returns to backers in terms of their being able to be attached, or be seen to be attached, to particular initiatives and activities.

Specific Financial Measures

Bearing all of the above in mind, the following may be measured.

Income

- *Income per employee:* this should include all the employees of the particular organization and not just the salesforce, production line or other sharp-end or front-line operators.

- *Income per customer:* by which the total income over a period is measured against the numbers of customers.

- *Income per offering:* either on an individual, product mix or product range basis.

- *Income per outlet:* in whatever the terms the outlet is defined by the particular organization (e.g. the office, the sales person, the department store, the airliner, the restaurant).

- *Income per square foot, per square metre, per product stack:* this can also be developed to cover individual premises and total premises owned.

- *Income per location:* having regard to the relative levels of prosperity, disposable income and propensity to spend of the local client base served.

Each of these items may also be represented as profit (profit per employee, per customer, per outlet, per offering, per square metre).

Financial measures may also be expressed in terms of the following.

* *Volume sales:* per product, per product cluster, per product range; volume sales per square foot, per outlet; volume sales per member of staff may also be calculated and, again, this should include everyone employed by the organization.

* *Density/frequency of usage:* this especially applies to sports, healthcare, hotel facilities, public transport, bank cashpoints, commercial durables such as photocopiers and faxes.

* *Longevity of usage:* this can usefully be applied to private transport, public transport, consumer durables, clothing, furniture, white goods.

* *Speed of turnover:* this is a statistical measure; however, calculation of this indicates the level of finance necessary to support the requirement to keep everything fully stocked.

Costs

Cost targets may be appropriate in relation to earnings, profits and activity volumes so that a cost (normally VC) per product, per product range, may be established and related to total income. Fixed costs may also be calculated in order to assess the amount that has to be sustained and supported in terms of equipment costs; capital charges; administrative and bureaucratic overheads; working methods; personnel, marketing and distribution charges; purchasing, lease and rental. Costs per employee, per department, per total square metre, per premises may also be calculated.

Notes

1. *Percentages*
   It is useful to know different percentage calculations, especially costs as a percentage of total income; percentage levels of profit; percentage returns on investment. Their best use is to indicate levels of business necessary to sustain effective, successful and profitable activity. Their worst use is when they become driving forces for performance targets without being set in the full operational context.

2.   *Comparisons*
         Comparisons are useful in that most organizations require some understanding of where they stand and how they operate in relation to others in their sector. From this, they may gain some knowledge as to whether there is any scope for improvement over all, or in particular activities.

         An understanding of comparisons is vital in the area of pricing and customer satisfaction. Customers may go to a top-quality operator and pay any price necessary rather than receive an inadequate offering at a lower price, for example.

         Comparisons may also be usefully made in the measurement of output, volume, profit margins and turnover, but care has to be taken that like is truly being compared with like. For example, in 1993, Honda UK declared a profit of £300 per car produced. This could be compared to the figure given by the exclusive Morgan Motor Company of £2,500 profit per car. However, they are not comparable operators. They do not serve the same market.

         Problems with comparisons also arise from taking comfort from general and bland statements such as: 'We are no worse than anyone else in the sector', or 'We are tenth out of 47 companies measured in the sector'. Such statements appear in industrial trade media and company annual reports. They should always be treated with the deepest suspicion. At the very least, they should always be a trigger for further inquiry and assessment for the true meaning of the comparison. All organizations ultimately have to have their own distinctive capability to exist independently.

3.   *Depreciation*
         Depreciation is an accounting convention used quite legitimately to write off the costs of specific investments against income over a future period. Its greatest danger is that it becomes a straitjacket in which organizations perceive themselves as being prevented from writing off particular equipment when it suddenly becomes obsolete.

4.   *Replacement*
         Technological advance, especially production and information technology, is so rapid that it becomes increasingly necessary to replace equipment before the end of its projected useful life. In most cases, this is a consequence of being in a particular sector or line of activity. While the need to invest in new technology and equipment is an obligation represented by a fixed cost, the true nature and extent of this fixed cost may not always be known.

5.   *Overdrafts*
Reference was made above to the use of bank loans and overdrafts as a source of funding. The ideal use of overdrafts is purely to finance short-term cashflow problems.

Ratios

Ratios are used by managers to identify, establish and measure particular performance aspects in a certain way. The results and outcomes, and the level and quality of performance that they indicate, contribute to management knowledge and information, and become part of the process of assessment and evaluation.

The most important ratios are as follows.

•   The profit ratio: net profit over total sales times a hundred indicates percentage net return. This can be calculated for total activities and for products and product clusters.

•   Selling costs: selling costs over total sales times a hundred indicates percentage consumed on sales costs. This may also be calculated for total sales; sales of individual products or product clusters; and for locations and outlets. The same approach can be taken for energy, production, marketing, staff and distribution as a percentage of sales.

•   Assets and liabilities: assets over liabilities. This may be broken down into:

   – long-term assets over long-term liabilities;

   – current assets over current liabilities;

   – quickly realizable assets over current liabilities (which is sometimes called the quick ratio or 'the asset test').

•   Debtors and creditors: debtors over creditors indicates whether an organization is paying out its bills more quickly than it is receiving its payments, or vice versa.

•   *Return on capital employed (ROCE):* profit before tax over capital employed gives rate of return on the investment.

These have to be seen in context. For example, while a quick ratio may show that a company could not easily cover its current liabilities, if these are not to be called in this does not matter. Returns on capital employed have to be seen in the broader context, and this is discussed further in the next chapter.

Budgets

Budgets are most effective when they are concentrated on the allocation and use of variable costs – above all, materials and other resource usage in departments and functions that change according to the level of activities.

A budget is a plan (with sub-plans) constituting part of the process of controlling levels of expenditure in departments, divisions and functions, and on projects and initiatives. The purpose is to provide an accurate picture of where and how resources are being used and the speed and frequency of this, and to form the basis for making future judgments on the levels of finance required to meet particular targets.

The budget enables specific analysis and evaluation of the accuracy of the resource allocation process and variances from it, and the explanation of why particular resource targets and projects have not been met. Budgets provide definable and quantifiable bases for corrective action – whether this is to do with profligacy in the use of organizational resources, or at the other extreme, where parts of an organization and particular activities are being starved of resources essential for effective operations.

At the core is the purpose for which the budget has been allocated. At the outset, this is usually based on an informed judgment of likely levels of resources required to do the job properly. Some measure of flexibility is also usual and this should include the ability to restrict as well as to expand or extend.

There should also be prescriptive, consultative and participative elements involved in the establishment of effective budgets. This should include the means of effective resource allocation and also ways of ensuring that all those involved in the implementation of particular activities understand fully the resource obligations and constraints under which they have to work. Even in areas of severe constraint – in public services for example – better responses will be generated if everyone concerned understands the nature and range of resource limitations.

Part of the budgeting process must also constitute the means for the identification of conflicting areas – conflicting and divergent resource demands and pressures for example – and their resolution and reconciliation. Both managers and accountants have a legitimate interest in this.

It is also essential to be able to reconcile control with flexibility, and this in turn requires a measure of leeway so that, for example, productive initiatives that need small extra amounts of resource in order for them to be fully successful can be accommodated without, at the same time, calling into question the whole credibility of the budgeting process. All budgeting systems must be specifically designed for the organization's initiatives, operations, projects, staff and facilities concerned.

Notes

1.   Serious problems have arisen in some sectors when budgets have included fixed cost allocations. In the National Health Service, one outcome of this has been that in some cases it is 'cheaper' and 'more cost effective' to have hospital wards closed than open, and staff idle on full pay, rather than busy and productive. In some schools and colleges it has been 'cheaper' and 'more cost effective' to hire teaching rooms at other venues than to use the institution's own premises which have consequently remained empty and idle. Budgeting approaches to some public road maintenance projects require a 'dash for work' at the end of the financial year (in January, February and March when the weather is at its worst for this kind of activity) to use up the budget.

2.   Serious problems occur more generally with 'using up the budget'. The most serious problem is when organizations, departments, divisions and functions go on a spending spree in order to use up their resources because they will be lost if not consumed.

Almost equally serious is the attitude taken by some organizations that, if all the resources in the budget are not consumed, then clearly the department, division or function concerned can operate on a reduced level of resources.

Both attitudes encourage waste rather than constraint and effective resource utilization. It is much better that organizations allow those responsible for establishing, maintaining and controlling budgets enough flexibility to get over these problems. In most cases, the only reason why these deadlines and cut-offs are used is because of a lack of capability and will on the part of those with overall responsibility to find something better.

Internal Markets

Internal markets are present in holding company structures, multinational organizations and health and other public services. They are a combination of the following elements:

- the distinction between purchasers and providers for the purposes of establishing a contracted arrangement;

- the establishment of a contracted agreement between purchasers and providers as the basis on which the relationship between the two is to be carried out in the future;

- the establishment of a price-service return, and the ways in which the services are to be paid for;

- agreeing quantity/volume, quality and timescale/deadlines criteria for each relationship established;

- the establishment of a system of transfer pricing which, in commercial organizations, enables the most advantageous currency to be used, and in public service organizations, requires a system of internal invoicing to be devised.

The overall purpose of any organizational internal market must be to ensure effectiveness of operation. This is based on the effectiveness and efficiency of resource identification, allocation and evaluation on the part of the control, administrative, finance and support functions of the organization.

Notes

1.   In public services, the greatest danger in creating internal markets is the creation of a substantial tier of administration. This has to be paid for, very often out of departmental budgets which are often already tight in the first place. In addition, they tend to create administrative workloads for professional and front-line operators and service providers which detract from the volume and quality of service available to client groups.

2.   The danger to private companies is that the reason for creating the internal market – overwhelmingly the capability of pricing in the most advantageous currency – is lost; and again, this leads to an additional burden of administration, and an additional head office/corporate function which is, again, a drain on the commercial activities of the organization.

Statistics

Mathematical and other numerical information is gathered and used as follows.

Human Resource Information

- General staffing information:

    - by occupation; by age; by gender; by disability; by ethnic origin.

    - by occupation; by department, division; by location; by function.

- Balance of staff numbers in primary and support functions.

- Balance of managerial and non-managerial staff.

- Rates of absenteeism, sickness, labour turnover by occupation, department, division, location and function.

- Rates of accidents, illnesses and injuries by occupation, department, division, location and function.

- Rates of disputes, grievances, strikes by occupation, department, division, location and function.

- Rates of disciplinary activity – above all, the use of disciplinary procedures – and the consequences arising from this (especially dismissal) by occupation, department, division, location and function.

These measures may be used as indicators of general levels of efficiency and effectiveness. They are also indicators of levels of motivation, morale and attitudes in the particular areas. Increases in each tend to indicate the presence of problems, or the presence of issues which, if not tackled, may become problems.

Levels of each are a matter for managerial judgment. There are no absolute right or wrong answers. However, it is always useful to bear the following in mind:

- every percentage point of absenteeism effectively adds one person per hundred to the payroll;

- it is possible to isolate the cost of recruiting particular members of staff and set this against the costs of retention and motivation;

- it is possible to calculate the cost per dispute, grievance, accident, injury and relate this to the cost of prevention;

- it is possible to establish a preferred level of absenteeism; however, this has to be supported by the appropriate management style and attention to staff.

Production Statistics

These may be measured as follows:

- output per production line; output per production shift; output per location; output per piece of equipment/technical unit/item of technology; output per member of staff;

- frequency/density of machine usage; operations as a percentage of total capacity/potential;

- time taken for components to be assembled into finished products; assembly time for given operations; product to market time; speed of product turnover; speed of component turnover;

- storage capacity; density of storage usage; delivery times for finished goods; delivery times for components;

- volume of supplier complaints; nature of supplier complaints; volume of customer complaints; nature of customer complaints;

- accident and injury statistics related to production methods.

Sales Statistics

These are measured as follows.

- sales as a percentage of prospects, leads, calls; sales by location; sales by outlet;

- sales per product; sales per product cluster; effect on total sales of introduction of new products/withdrawal of some products;

- volume of complaints; location of complaints; nature of complaints;

- creditor and debtor periods;

- salesforce accessibility;

- speed, frequency and density of sales – per product; per product cluster; per outlet; per location;

- sales by format – retail; wholesale; mail order and catalogue; newspaper and magazine;

- interrelationship of sales forms – e.g. are people attracted to buy from the shops because of the availability of catalogues and newspaper outlets;

- income per customer;

- nature of customer expenditure – cash, cheque, credit card, standing order, hire purchase, other finance plans.

Administration

This may be measured as follows:

- length of administrative procedures;

- purpose of administrative procedures; the extent to which procedures meet their purpose;

- volume of administration as a percentage of total workload;

- numbers of staff in support functions; percentage of staff in support functions;

- proportion of fixed costs allocated to administration;

- proportion of premises allocated to administration;

- information technology – availability of technology; expertise in technology; capacity of technology; desired use of technology;

- levels of business required to cover administration;

- cost of administration per member of staff; total cost of administration; total cost of administration as a proportion of total organizational cost.

Performance Measurement in Public Services

Public services are best measured as follows:

- accessibility of client groups, access to client groups; levels of satisfaction; nature of complaints; volume of complaints; location of complaints;

- levels of return/repeat calls necessary (e.g. hospitals, social services, social security); totality of service (e.g. if someone goes into hospital for one complaint and another is diagnosed, can this be treated on the spot or is a further appointment necessary);

- subsequent remedial action, levels and nature – e.g. extent to which adult literacy classes are required because the school system has failed people in the past;

- overall usage levels; demands for each service element;

- interrelationship of services – e.g. the extent to which crime levels rise because inadequate education/leisure services/facilities and amenities are provided;

- currency of equipment; currency of education, training, technological usage and awareness; adequacy of environment;

- desired waiting times; actual waiting times; access to experts;

- proportions of expenditure on administration, service provision, support functions.

Note

There is often a fundamental discrepancy between the nature of services and the political drives of those responsible for them. For example, education can take up to twenty years to complete, yet the Minister in charge needs to be able to demonstrate tangible and presentable results in months if not weeks. This also applies to health, social security and transport policies.

Performance Measures in the Not-for-Profit Sector

These are measured as follows:

- size of donor groups; location of donor groups; rates of donation; average donations;

- sources of all donations; proportions of each donation; core and peripheral donors;

- current nature of donations (e.g. cash, kind, standing order, time, effort); desired nature of donations;

- proportions of expenditure on client groups; desired levels of expenditure on client groups; feasible levels of expenditure on client groups;

- access to client groups; access of client groups to the organization.

Note

For both public services and the not-for-profit sector, the measures indicated under the above headings of human resource, production and sales can be easily translated into public service and not-for-profit equivalent terms.

Conclusions

All information, financial and statistical, must be capable of being used by managers and organizations as a contribution to the assessment of performance. This means that:

- historic and current information has to be complete and accurate – both the information itself and the methods used to collect, store, retrieve and present it must be suitable for the purposes of those who are to use it;

- all quantitative data is only of value if it is available in ways that the organization, and those within it, can understand and use;

- managers must have faith and confidence in the information received and the systems used.

The managerial approach, and the ability of managers to use information, begins where the role of those who produce it – accountants, economists, statisticians – ends. Accurate and useful judgment and evaluation is possible only on this basis. Under no circumstances are the figures a substitute for managerial decision-making. There are a range of other factors which have to be taken into account, and these are discussed in the next chapter.

4   Managerial aspects

Having identified the qualitative and quantitative measures of organizational performance, the main remaining points to address are who uses them, how to use them and points of inquiry for their application.

Who Uses Performance Measures?

Different groups of people, quite legitimately, measure organization and managerial performance. These are the stakeholders and interested parties. They hold varying types and degrees of influence and interest in the products and services, the ways of working, standards and their outcomes. They make their own judgments on successes and failures. They are as follows.

Stakeholders

- *The staff:* everyone who works for and in the organization, and who is therefore dependent upon it for income and spending power and, to a greater extent, for their standard and style of living. This also applies to subcontractors and other retainers, and to potential staff. It also covers trade unions, employers' and professional associations, and any others who have representative interests.

- *The community:* in which the staff live and work and in which the organization operates. All organizations have a basic general association with their communities. They provide work and resource for the community and therefore support other economic activities within it.

- *Social customers:* for example, charities, schools and hospitals which may approach the organization for sponsorship and support for social, educational, charitable and other worthy causes.

- *Shareholders:* the investors of money in an organization, in the expectation and anticipation of returns.

- *Other financial interests:* including backers, contributors, bankers, other loan-makers, venture capitalists, sponsors, city institutions and stock markets.

- *Suppliers of components and raw materials:* these have a vested interest in the continuing success of the organization, both in terms of continuity of this particular sphere of business and also in the gaining of a wider reputation for the performance of things which they supply; their long-term success is dependent upon that of the organizations to which they provide supplies.

- *The sectors and markets:* in which organizations offer their products and services for sale.

- *Distributors and agents:* who rely on their own position between particular organizations and the end users of the products or services.

- *Government departments and agencies:* with whom the organization comes into contact. For the public sector, government departments and agencies have a direct involvement in that they are the main backers and providers of resources. More generally, at the very least, this means legal and financial compliance.

- *Trade, market and employers' federations and associations.*

- *Competitors and offerers:* of alternative products and services. These have to be considered as stakeholders because the loss of a competitor in a sector may not only lead to greater opportunities for those remaining in it, but this may also lead to its destabilization.

- *Lobbyists, vested interest groups and other influential groups:* related to the location and nature of activities, the ways in which those activities are carried out, and again, those with a direct interest in the supply and distribution.

- *Those who set distinctive social, economic, political, legal and ethical standards.*

- *Customers, clients and other product and service users:* and potential customers, clients, product and service users.

Interested Parties

Interested parties are those who come into contact with an organization or its products in more general ways. They may be regular, occasional, influential or uninfluential.

Regular interested parties are normally those who have continued indirect contact with an organization, for example those who regularly pass a shop, bus or railway station on the way to work or who must cross a park during the course of their normal activities or regularly pass a pub or club at a specific time. By doing this, they form a strong and/or dominant impression of it that nevertheless almost certainly does not give the full picture. This does not prevent them from passing their own judgment.

Occasional interested parties are those who have this form of contact on a less continuous basis.

Influential interested parties are those able to pass key or critical judgments as the result of their regular or occasional contact. For example, a councillor who witnesses rowdy behaviour outside a pub or club on the only occasion in the past five years that he/she has been near it may have an adverse view the next time its licence comes up for renewal. Or a journalist may use his/her professional position to pronounce on the overall state of an organization based only on this level of contact.

Uninfluential interested parties contribute to the fund of general knowledge, perception and prejudice held about organizations in their communities through conversations, and sometimes also through writing letters, occasional visits and other general contacts.

Everyone who comes into contact with an organization, and its products and services, therefore assesses it in some way or another.

How Is Performance Measured?

The most important fact is continuity – in the assessment, measurement and appraisal of performance, drawing conclusions on a regular basis so that a full watching brief is maintained, and so that early warning is given of things that may be going wrong.

Ideally, this is punctuated with regular team, peer and organizational meetings arranged for the specific purpose of reporting on performance. Given that no activity takes place in total isolation, performance reporting must consider the effectiveness of working relationships and coordination of activities, as well as the legitimate interests of those both within the organization and outside.

Organizations and their managers should also regularly review the actual measures and indicators used and the ways in which they are used to ensure that these continue to be valid, reliable and capable of demonstrating what they are supposed to demonstrate. This extends to received wisdom,

generalizations and self-perceptions, both from inside and outside the organization, as well as more specific measures. As examples, the following questions may be asked:

- 'Why do we have performance-related pay?' – 'Because it motivates the staff and targets performance.'

- 'Why do my staff complain that I am inaccessible? I am always consulting with them.'

These examples, and others raised in exactly the same way, need full and careful analysis and consideration. Otherwise, the points raised simply become institutionalized. One or two such features are likely not to be too damaging (though they should always nevertheless be remedied). Each feeds off others, however, and too many such questions nearly always reflect complacency within managerial ranks. For these (and all other such questions), quantitative and qualitative approaches are required to gather real information, and they then have to be considered from the required managerial standpoint. In turn, it is consequently essential to identify the right points of inquiry for all managers and groups of managers as a check on their own performance, and on their contribution to that of the organization as a whole.

Points of Inquiry

These are treated from two different angles:

- those that apply to each function;

- considerations of costs, benefits, risks, value and time.

Functional Issues

Human Resource Management

- The numbers of strikes, disputes and grievances; movements in the numbers of disciplinaries and dismissals; the extent and movements in the operation of disciplinary, grievance and disputes procedures.

- Movements in the numbers of accidents and injuries; movements in the numbers of self-certificated absenteeism.

- Levels of disputes and grievances among those who enjoy perceived high levels of job satisfaction and job security.

- Movements in staff turnover; movements (especially decreases) in organizational, departmental, divisional and functional staff stability.

- Increases in administration and support functions at the expense of front-line operations; increases in the administration and reporting workload placed on front-line operations.

- Pay differentials between the top and bottom of the organization.

- Pay increases are awarded to those at the top of the organization at the expense of those at the bottom.

- Those at the top of the organization receive benefits (e.g. cars, computers, mobile phones) based on status rather than operational necessity.

- Pay awards, promotion and other enhancements are given for administrative and procedural efficiency rather than direct performance effectiveness.

- Performance-related pay is achieved by those in head office and other support functions, and not by those at the front line.

- Those at the top of the organization are treated more favourably than those at the bottom in matters of discipline, grievance handling, disputes.

- Those in support functions are treated more favourably generally than those at the front line.

- Discipline, grievance and dispute problems are institutionalized and not resolved, and these procedures take a long time to work through.

- Pay awards are paid in arrears rather than on time.

Production

- Production targets, especially where production output bears no relationship to targets set; this is as much a cause for concern when targets are far exceeded as when they are not met.

- Production, volume and quality, especially where these fall short of projections.

- Increases in customer complaints about one aspect of product performance, for example failure of one component.

- Increases in customer complaints about total product performance.

- Increases in customer complaints about packaging, delivery, appearance, durability and after-sales service.

- Increases in customer recalls because the organization has found the product to be faulty.

- Increases in supply problems, access to components and raw materials.

- Increases in internal disputes between those responsible for gaining raw materials, those responsible for direct production, and those responsible for sales and distribution.

- Increases in unit costs, variable costs.

- Inability of fixed costs to sustain commercial operations and activities.

- Production and information technology is not/no longer suitable for the purposes for which it was bought or designed.

- Difficulties in use of production and information technology; lack of user-friendliness.

- Maintenance issues and problems with production and information technology; balance of preventative and emergency/crisis maintenance.

- Extent and nature of training offered, demanded and available; extent of obligation to understand this/make it available.

- Identifying where blockages occur, why, what causes them (e.g. component and raw materials supplies, availability of packaging); their effects on total effectiveness.

- New products and developments: proportion of new products that get to market; actual and required research, development capability and expertise; research and development as a percentage of total organizational activities/fixed costs.

Marketing and Sales

- Currency and effectiveness of marketing information and research.

- Sources of customer satisfaction and dissatisfaction; the benefits that customers expect to accrue from purchase/ownership of the products and services; the benefits that actually accrue as the result, and where the differences between the two lie.

- Changes in customer perceptions – especially from positive to negative (though a change from negative to positive may cause increases in demand with which the organization is unable to cope).

- Organizational perceptions of 'good value' are seen by customers as 'cheap'.

- Benefits to customers perceived by producers are not/no longer perceived to be benefits by customers themselves.

- Marketing and promotional campaigns do not have the desired/projected effects on sales.

- Marketing and promotional campaigns cause major problems due to lack of full investigation, assessment and analysis.

- Lack of full market knowledge and understanding – often based on market research that generates 'generally favourable impressions' (i.e. 'would you buy' rather than 'will you buy').

- Poor public relations which is usually symptomatic of organizational lack of sureness, capability or faith in what it is doing.

- Required and desired images and identity, not generated by marketing and advertising campaigns.

- Marketing rebounds – unlooked for (usually negative) consequences of marketing, advertising and promotion activities; this may also be a problem when very high notes are scored and the organization is unable to satisfy increased demand.

Communications

- Quality and volume of written, oral, formal and informal communications.

- Extent and content of grapevine.

- Extent and nature of communication blockages and misunderstandings.

- Frequency and value of team, group, department, division and functional meetings; their agenda; outputs and outcomes.

- Extent and use of formal communication channels; length of time taken; general effectiveness; effects on operations, administration, decision-making processes.

- Extent and use of informal channels; length of time taken; general effectiveness; specific effects on operations, administration and decision-making processes.

- Effectiveness of formal and established systems – especially of consultation, participation and access to organization information.

- Nature and value of information to which different groups have access.

- Organization and operational confidentiality; perceived organizational and operational confidentiality.

- Information systems: ease of access to information; capacity for the acquisition, storage, retrieval, analysis and processing of information.

- Visibility and accessibility of managers and supervisors.

- Language used: the simpler and more direct this is, the more likely it is that what is said will be understood.

- Integrity of communications: the extent to which they mean what they say and say what they mean.

- Hidden/secondary agenda: the messages that are actually received by those receiving them; the messages that the organization is actually putting across; as reflected in the nature and language of what is said and written.

Each of these elements is to be considered in relation to all stakeholders and interested parties, and this means assessing the quality of external communications as well as internal.

Organizational

- Poor quality and volume of communications.

- One-way (or perceived one-way) style of communications where orders are handed down from on high.

- Lack of adequate consultation.

- Increases in awards against the organization by industrial tribunals, the health and safety executive, trading standards.

- Increases in adverse publicity and media coverage; decreases in favourable publicity and media coverage.

- Increased psychological distance between levels of the hierarchy and between different functions.

- Presence of physical distance between managers and those at the front line; lack of recognition of the effects of this and of problems caused/inherent.

- Lack of autonomy on the part of those working away from head office (see *£9.99 syndrome* example, Appendix); constant need to refer back to head office.

- Bad/negative/adversarial management style: often exacerbated by priorities on administration and procedural efficiency rather than operational success.

- Lack of clarity of overall purpose; lack of attention to subordinate goals, aims and objectives.

- Poor organizational standing in its community: often caused by a combination of being a known or perceived bad employer and using production processes which are known or perceived to harm or pollute the environment. This is, in turn, enhanced when the organization refuses to take its full place in its community (see *PR at Selafield* example, Appendix).

- Inaccessibility of managers and supervisors; lack of communication and coordination between functional and operational groups, departments and divisions.

- Balances and proportions of front line with support and administration activities; and balances and proportions of resources allocated to each.

- Complexity/simplicity of procedures; accessibility and understanding of procedures; time taken and resources used in their operation.

- Extent of crisis management; the matters that fall into the 'crisis' category.

- Attention to work patterns and methods; extent of alienation, divisive work practices; attention to job and work improvement methods.

- Extent and prevalence of 'them and us' divides between: head office and outlying functions; primary and support functions; managers and staff.

- Organizational politics: identifying where the real power and influence lies; why; whether this is appropriate; the extent and influence of over-mighty subjects and over-mighty departments (see example, Appendix).

Costs and Benefits

Cost-benefit analysis is a straightforward ready-reckoner for the assessment and measurement of initiatives. It identifies those elements that require further or more detailed consideration in advance of implementation. All the costs and charges that could possibly be incurred are identified and then set against all the values or benefits that will be accrued once it is undertaken and completed. The following areas are considered.

- Defining the costs and benefits to be assessed.

- Short, medium and long termism: the time periods over which costs are to be incurred and over which the results and benefits are to accrue.

- Values: to be seen from both economic and income generation points of view; also in wider terms – the knock-on effects anticipated, and other opportunities for the future.

- Priorities: what needs tackling first and why; the logic for this; other implications for the organization.

- Any implications for the wider impact of particular initiatives – effects on resources, current and existing activities, and so on.

- Risk and uncertainty.

- Strategic aspects/overviews – the effects that particular initiatives have on current market position, current product/service range; this may also be seen in terms of pump-priming, pioneering and innovative activity.

- Relative valuation – different costs and benefits at different times, the frequency with which costs and benefits are to occur, the intervals at which they are to occur, and how these are to be reconciled.

- The balance between income and expenditure – seen in both the narrow context of given initiatives, and also the wider effects on organizational activities.

This provides for a broader and more detailed background analysis than a pure inquiry into functional activities. The functional questions should still be asked, and where appropriate, particular quantitative and qualitative aspects addressed also. An assessment of costs and benefits should feature in the discussions of any major undertaking as part of the target setting, feasibility and initiative design stages.

Value

The purpose of analysing value is to establish where the elements and activities that add value to the organization's offerings lie, and conversely where value is lost or deducted. Analysing value may be related to products, services and offerings; all the departments, divisions and functions; strategic

and operational elements; purchasing, supply, input, process, output and distribution; and administration and support.

The components of value are:

- length, frequency and intensity of usage;

- depreciation/appreciation of resources;

- feelings of esteem and worth;

- feelings of exclusivity, luxury, desirability and pride;

- returns on investment, activity, energy and effort;

- particular individual demands and requirements;

- maintenance, repair and replacement; development and improvement.

Each aspect of organizational performance, as well as the use of products and services by customers, can then be assessed using each of these elements. This enables attention to be switched to those areas where value is being lost and not maximized. It also enables the strengths of each activity to be assessed in terms of the positive benefits that it brings to the organization.

Time

Organizations and their managers must be able to distinguish between what constitutes long-term, medium-term and short-term time in their own situations.

It is impossible to prescribe any given periods of time for each. To do so denies the variances that actually exist between all organizations and within all organizations in the pursuit of their own defined aims and objectives. There are sectoral variances that have to be considered: one person's long term, is another's instant. Matters relating to lead times have also to be considered: it takes much longer to get some activities and projects launched than others, while others have to be carried out instantly if they are to have any value at all.

It is therefore much better to see these measures of time in the following terms.

- *Short-term:* that which is achievable and measurable in precise terms. It will be precisely targeted and subject to regular review, discussion and appraisal. The deadline for completion will be 'nearer to hand'.

- *Medium-term:* that which is clearly achievable and measurable, precisely targeted, and subject to regular review and monitoring as it unfolds. The approach here is more flexible than for the short term, without losing sight of the overall purpose or desired and envisaged outcome. Again, the date will be a clearly recognized target.

- *Long-term:* a clear understanding of direction, the shape of things to come, and things that are getting underway or being researched and commissioned. Long-term time periods have three main values – precise initiatives eventually become medium term and then short term; it is necessary to secure the long-term future of the organization; and it is also necessary to balance a clear long-term purpose with the need not to get bogged down in too much detail of a future which cannot possibly be measured accurately.

Time also has to be considered over periods that balance and reflect the need for successful and effective long-term performance with the demands of principle stakeholders for results – for example, government departments expect to see instant cost cuts in public services; shareholders expect returns on their investment at least once a year in the form of dividends.

The balance between activity time and maintenance/repair/development time must also be assessed. With activity time, it is useful to be able to distinguish between:

- *development time* – the time taken to produce and test new inventions and their components;

- *research time* – taken to establish measures of market size, demand, availability and nature;

- *production time* – covering all aspects of the manufacture of products and the totality of the components of services;

- *distribution and delivery time* – the time taken to get goods and services to customers, clients and users;

- *review time* – the time taken to monitor and assess the effects of particular initiatives, and the overall success and effectiveness of performance.

The overwhelming need is to set realistic and achievable objectives within whatever timeframe is considered. It is also essential to consider the wider behavioural point – that it is much better to set long timescales and deliver early, rather than short timescales and deliver late.

Organization Politics

Individuals and groups have to survive long enough to become successful and effective operators. They have therefore to be able to make use of systems, procedures, practices and support mechanisms. People have to develop their own format for the niches that they occupy and the roles and functions that they carry out in order to maximize their chances of being successful and effective.

This means attention to the following.

- Developing approaches based on a combination of role, function and personality; and this means, in turn, developing measures of trust, warmth and liking as part of professional and operational dealings.

- Developing approaches based on individual influence – recognizing the nature of the influence and the ability to present it in ways useful to others in the organization.

- Developing networks of professional, personal and individual contacts, and using these as a means of gaining fresh insights and approaches to issues and problems.

- Developing funds of bargaining chips – equipment, information, resources and expertise – which can, if necessary, be used in trade-offs and for mutual advantage and satisfaction.

- Developing a clarity of thought around the entire aspect of organizational operations and activities. This is based, on the one hand, on what is important, urgent and of value, and to whom, and on the other, on what facilitates progress and what hinders or blocks it.

The organization itself, and those responsible for its governance, direction and performance, need to recognize the nature and prevalence of the different forms of political activity. This includes the effects on operations, effectiveness and success. Some in-fighting and competition may not be apparent to those at the top. They may also not perceive that their activities,

those achievements for which they issue rewards and punishments, or the bases on which resources are allocated, create strife and dissention elsewhere.

Organization politics are sometimes encouraged and used as forms of control by those at the top. They observe the effects of encouraging this form of behaviour in terms of giving direction and focus to different groups and individuals.

Teams and groups that depend on particular forms, resources and support for their continued well-being and existence need to establish relationships with those who hand these out. The basis of this is likely to include matters such as support for the backers in other initiatives, sharing the merits and glories of success, and distance from any apparent failure.

Individuals need to be able to create physical and psychological space in order to be able to pursue their own aims, and practise and develop their expertise. Ideally, this will accord with the organization's overall direction, though even where this is so, a certain amount of politicking and lobbying is normally required.

Departments, divisions and functions become involved in organizational politics overwhelmingly because of the need to compete for resources and to maintain their own reputation and standing. This is at its most extreme where competition for resources and reputation is based on the 'distributive' principle – whereby one succeeds at the expense of others.

Understanding, surviving and operating in organizations stems from this assessment.

Confidence and Expectations

Everyone who comes into contact with an organization expects to have confidence in it – confidence in the strength and quality of the overall relationship; confidence in its products and services; confidence in its continuity, reliability and stability; confidence in its continuing success and effectiveness.

People join and work for organizations, make purchases, and avail themselves of services, with certain expectations in mind. They anticipate that their expectations will be fulfilled. Problems occur when these expectations are not fulfilled. Levels of expectation are set by a variety of needs.

- *For staff:* there is the need to be well rewarded; to gain job satisfaction, fulfilment, development and achievement; to be associated with a positive and prestigious organization or occupation; to be valued, respected and esteemed.

- *For shareholders and backers:* there is a need to receive regular positive returns on investment; to receive specific dividends and other benefits as the result of investment.

- *Customers, consumers, clients and users:* these expect satisfaction and utility from the products and services; in many cases, they also expect esteem, respect and value to be enhanced.

- *Communities:* these expect to feel pleased and proud to have certain organizations established and working in among them.

Problems arise when a lack of confidence sets in and when expectations are not met. Part of the wider assessment of managerial performance is therefore to understand what the nature of confidence is and what the expectations of the particular stakeholders and interested parties are, and to take steps to ensure that, as far as possible, these are satisfied.

Conclusions

Each of these elements and factors is an essential and legitimate area for managerial inquiry when assessing either total organization performance, or parts and features of it. Most of these elements and factors are interrelated. Several appear under different headings. Others are directly consequential – for example, it is impossible to have good and positive organizational attitudes without having clear standards established by top management. Taken altogether they reflect the fact that the performance of every organization, and every department, division and function within it, can always be improved.

This also underlines the complexity of measuring performance successfully. This is true even where supposedly simple or direct targets have been set – for example, a simple increase in the outputs of a production line. Before such a decision can be taken, it has to be ensured that adequate volumes of components and supplies are available (or can be made available), that they can be stored, that any additional staff or overtime can be paid for, and that the increased output can be packaged, stored, distributed – and sold. It may be that such an increase adversely affects morale (for example, the need for additional production may be the latest in a long series of crises), or it may send morale sky-high, and this may subsequently lead to complacency if a positive, yet realistic, approach is not maintained.

So the role of the professional manager – whether chief executive officer, director, top, middle, junior or front-line and supervisory – is to understand this, and to continue to attend to each of the elements and factors indicated. This is equally important when things are going well, as the reasons why success is being achieved can be fully explained and understood. When things do go wrong, and problems begin to arise, they can be identified early and nipped in the bud. This, in turn, is best achieved if all managers understand the full range of inquiry that they need to make, and that nothing happens in isolation.

5 Conclusions

The measurement of organizational and managerial performance is complex and requires a high level of contextual knowledge and understanding, as well as the capability to choose the right qualitative and quantitative measures, and the required points of inquiry.

From this, managers are able to identify what contributes to successful, effective and profitable performance for their own organization, and that part of it for which they are responsible. They can also pinpoint:

- those activities that contribute to effective, successful and profitable organizational performance, the extent and nature of that contribution, and their effects upon each other;

- those activities that do not make any direct contribution to performance;

- those activities that detract from successful and effective performance, that destroy and damage it, that dilute its effectiveness;

- diversions from purpose, blockages and barriers to progress;

- the proportion and balance of steady-state activities with crisis handling.

Constraints

It is necessary to recognize the range of parties, both internal and external, who have a legitimate interest in the organization, who measure it for success or failure, and the measures that they bring to bear from their own point of view. Long-term viability is much more likely where the concerns of each group can be addressed and reconciled successfully. One of the main tasks of top managers is to recognize the nature and legitimacy of the interests of the different stakeholder groups and interested parties, and to take steps to see that these are widely understood and satisfied as far as possible.

From this approach to performance, assessment and measurement comes a clear understanding of what the organization and its managers can control and influence, and what cannot be controlled or influenced. For example, it may not be possible to suppress a glut of bad or negative publicity and

adverse media coverage. However, organizations can influence future coverage by responding as positively as possible in the circumstances, and by using this as a springboard to generate long-term positive interest.

Similarly, it is also not possible to control particular social, legal, economic and political constraints; but it is possible to recognize and understand the extent of their influence, and to work within them. It may also not be possible in the short to medium term at least to influence the size or nature of markets served; and again, it is possible to recognize these specific constraints, and to provide products and services as successfully, effectively and profitably as possible within them.

Politics

Within organizations, managers have to survive as well as operate. All organizations have their own politics and their constituent parts of alliances, hook-ups, associations, lobbies and pressure groups. Individual managers must understand their position within these, the extent of their influence and specific limitations imposed on their ability to act.

The wider concern for all organizations is when their political systems become the overwhelming reason for there being large numbers of staff. This is prevalent at corporate head offices and throughout public service administrative functions. Symptoms of this are rewarding staff for efficient political rather than operational capacity and achievement. In the worst cases, top managers encourage this through systems of resource bidding and allocation, in which they play off departments, divisions and functions against each other, overtly rewarding some functions and individuals at the expense of others.

In the long term, this is fatal to organizational health and well-being. In the shorter term, individuals nevertheless concentrate on using the political system to their own advantage to gain personal and professional, or occupational, recognition and advancement, and ultimately to build up their own reputation and perceived achievement to a sufficient extent that it is possible to remove themselves altogether.

Visibility and Access

The greater the degree of visibility and access, both between supervisors and subordinates, and also across functions, departments and divisions, the greater the likelihood of excellent high levels of performance over the long term.

Visibility and access reinforce quality of working and interpersonal relationships, and these in turn, lead to early recognition and attention to problems when they arise. This applies to both production and human resource issues.

Visibility and accessibility are affected adversely by:

- *physical distance:* when the superior is based at a different location from the subordinate;

- *psychological distance:* which is caused by behavioural barriers such as status, job titles, formal modes of address.

The lesson is to recognize and understand the nature of these barriers and their effects on performance. Once they have been considered, it may remain in the organization's best interests to retain them. Only once they have been assessed, and the reasons for their existence clarified, however, can a true and valid judgment take place.

The Working Environment

It is essential to create a working environment where high and effective levels of performance can be generated in the first place, as well as the capability to understand and evaluate it.

The ideal working environment consists of the following.

- High levels of autonomy, the ability to self-manage and self-organize; this also includes group responsibility for self-regulation and self-discipline. This encourages the fast and effective resolution of problems, and a commitment to dealing with issues before they become problems.

- Clear and unambiguous performance targets, capable of achievement and related to overall organization purpose; understood, accepted and committed to by all concerned.

- Full responsibility for all aspects of production and output process, quality assurance, customer relations and complaints.

- Job titles do not include references to status differentials or trappings, or other elements of psychological distance.

- Team-based reward systems available and payable to everyone who contributes, based on percentages of salary rather than occupational differentials.

- The open approach to environment layout (no individual offices, trappings, barriers, or other factors of physical and psychological distance); self-commitment for the whole team; open communications; high quality communications; open approaches to problems and issues; open airing of grievances and concerns; no culture of blame.

- A federal relationship to the core organization with reporting relationships based on monitoring, review and evaluation of production and output targets and task-based indicators.

- Supportive general management style – rather than directive, bureaucratic or administrative.

- Quick and easy access to maintenance and support staff when necessary; attention to preventative maintenance as well as repairs.

- Full flexibility of work, multi-skilling and interchangeability between task roles.

- Continuous development of skills, knowledge, qualities, capabilities and expertise.

- Continuous attention to performance quality and output.

- Continuous attention to production, quality, volume and time.

- Continuous attention to high levels of service and satisfaction.

- Continuous attention to all stakeholder and interested party interests.

- High levels of involvement, confidence, respect and enthusiam among group members, both towards each other and the work.

- Attention to equipment and technology to ensure that this continues to be suitable and capable of producing that which is. required to the stated and expected standards of volume, quality and time.

- Simple, clear and supportive policies and procedures covering organizational rules and regulations.

- Continuous monitoring and review to ensure that aims and objectives are pursued, and that group activities accord with these.

Finally, only by measuring and assessing all aspects of organization performance, and relating these to the broader context in which activities take place, can actual success and failure be judged. It enables statements such as 'This was pretty successful' or 'That was a total disaster' to be further quantified and examined, and reasons found. It indicates areas where improvements can, and should, be made. It is the key to effective long-term resource utilization. It is essential if lessons are to be learned from the past and current range of activities, so that the future may be better prepared for. Above all, it is essential that every organization and every manager learns to do it, and do it well. In all spheres of activity, the best are doing it already, and they are therefore providing the standards against which everyone else is judged.

Appendix

Aims and Objectives

The following examples are included to serve as illustrations of some of the points made in the text, and also to encourage broad and critical thinking in the area.

1.   **Performance targets in public services**

The main problem to be addressed lies in the establishment of a valid standpoint from which to measure the performance of these services. This has to be reconciled with immediate short-term needs, drives and directions of politicians and service managers. There are also often historical bases, resource constraints and social pressures which all have to be accommodated.

The knowledge, expertise, judgment, attributes and qualities of the public service manager become critical. These form the context in which the following broad and narrow perspectives can be taken.

*   *Broad:* the state of the work environment – the school, classroom, library, hospital ward, laboratory, prison; the availability, use, value, quality and appropriateness of equipment to service users and consumers; cleanliness, warmth and comfort; general ambience; professionalism of staff; currency of professional expertise; interaction of staff with consumers; prioritization of activities; resource effectiveness, efficiency, adequacy and usage.

*   *Narrow:* application of absolute standards of service delivery; speed of response to consumers; nature and content of response to users; nature and volume of complaints, failures and shortcomings; attitudes of service users to providers and vice versa; acceptance of professional responsibility of standards; acceptance of professional development; personal commitment.

This is the context for setting specific aims and objectives in public services. It requires concentration on the output of specific services – and has no reference to inter-functional comparisons or league tables. This is the best basis of judgment and evaluation of performance for such services. It is to be carried out by service

experts and analysts (in the same way as commercial and business analysts and experts carry out the evaluation of private sector company performance).

Example

For the period 1993–94, the UK Scottish Office was required to meet the following target:

- that no more than 2.5 category B prisoners per thousand be lost.

Given that there were 3,000 prisoners in this category, the absolute requirement was that no more than 7.5 prisoners be lost in fact.

Nobody seemed to be able to explain how the target had been devised, who devised it, or why it was considered the right way of measuring this activity.

2.   **Sectoral norms and expectations**

When Japanese car and electrical goods companies first commenced operations in the West in the late 1960s and early 1970s, they brought hitherto unknown standards of quality and output. This resulted in the indigenous operators losing market share and having to respond through investment, training and development. It also became apparent that there was great scope for improvement in these sectors in Western Europe and North America. The Japanese initiatives also transformed the general expectations of performance and value for money in the sectors. Not only were the Western companies not seen to be performing but, indeed, the customer base was turning away from them and to the new superior product.

It underlines the need for continued attention to market conditions, consumer expectations, the global nature of business – and that consumer perceptions, expectations and requirements can change at very short notice.

3.   **Exit interviews**

A useful tool in assessing the reasons for labour turnover is the exit interview. Properly structured and targeted, it gives precise reasons why people are moving on. The results can then be analysed and used to understand:

- those labour movements that can be controlled and those that cannot;

- particular problems in particular functions, areas, departments and divisions;

- whether the organization is being used as a springboard to better things elsewhere;

- to break down the leave of population by age, location, sector, qualification, expertise and so on.

It is much better to have this information to hand in this format than to simply look at labour turnover figures and assess them for 'general acceptability' or otherwise.

4.   **£9.99 syndrome**

£9.99 syndrome occurs where managers with high levels of responsibility have one silly blockage placed on their activities. It is called the £9.99 syndrome because one of the silliest examples occurred in a factory in North Eastern England where a manager on £80,000 a year, with responsibility for a £500 million activity, nevertheless had to refer back to head office for expenditure above £10. This situation was aggravated by the fact that in the case in question, permission to grant this level of expenditure very often took several days to come through and had always to be confirmed in writing.

5.   **Public relations at Selafield**

The Windscale nuclear processing plant and nuclear power station in North Eastern England, had its name changed to Selafield following a series of environmental and operational disasters.

Other than among its immediate community (for which it provided employment), it enjoyed wide negative reputation and connotations. It addressed this through a series of carefully designed media events, supported with public relations materials. It concentrated on education for those still at school and college. It opened its doors to the general public who were able to go on guided tours of the establishment – the only areas restricted were those in which access was also restricted to the staff because of the high levels of radiation.

This activity at least enabled the previous negative coverage and perception to be fought off. While the establishment is still not seen in the highest possible terms, its reputation has increased greatly.

6.   **Over-mighty subjects**

The phrase 'over-mighty subjects' was first coined to describe the noblemen whom Henry VIII used to help him govern the outlying parts of the kingdom. Because of the nature of communications and transport at the time, he could not easily get to those parts of the kingdom. He therefore had to patronize those noblemen, and this effectively meant that they governed in his stead. It was also apparent that he could not govern the country – nor retain his throne – without their continued support.

In current business terms, the phrase is used to describe those managers and technical experts without whom distant or highly sophisticated functions and activities could not be carried out.

A recent and notorious example of this was Nick Leeson, who was a senior employee of Barings Bank in Singapore from 1991–94. The bank effectively required him to manage their Singapore operations to the best of his capability. The subsequent collapse of the bank proved their powerlessness to restrain his activities.

Equivalent employees are found in public services – especially among those officials who enjoy high levels of political patronage.

7.   **Confidence and expectations**

Leaders and top managers may expect to lose their jobs very quickly, if not instantly, once confidence has been lost and once they do not measure up to the expectations of organization stakeholders. As examples:

*   Margaret Thatcher, UK Prime Minister from 1979–90, won a vote of confidence from her Party in November 1990, but not by a large enough majority. She lost her job four days later.

*   John Akers resigned from his position as Chief Executive at IBM in January 1993. This was after the company had declared the then highest ever corporate loss of $5 billion, and followed this with a staff resizing programme for the first time.

- James Robinson stood down from the position of Chief Executive at American Express in January 1993, following the declaration of greatly reduced operating profits for 1992.

In each case, the person named left their job before they had intended to do so and as a consequence of the circumstances noted. This does not mean that the results declared were their fault. In each case, however, the sacrifice of them for the greater good of the organization in question was felt to be the most appropriate course of action.

8.   **The grapevine**

The grapevine is the difference between what people know, and what they want to know. If organization communications are adequate and effective, then the grapevine is confined to general chit-chat and gossip.

A sure indication that organization communications are bad, ineffective and inadequate is where the grapevine is used to make up the difference between what people do know and what they do not. This is a certain way of spreading rumours. It also adds fuel to the fire of disputes and grievances. People take sides in each, and minor problems quickly get out of hand and become trials of strength.

9.   **Timing**

Co-Steel Plc, of Sheerness, Kent, gave notice of instant derecognition of their trade union and radical changes to the ways of working of industrial relations late one Friday afternoon. The staff were briefed on the Friday afternoon and given notes and leaflets to take home with them to be read and digested over the weekend. The union was told to clear its offices immediately. Staff had all weekend to get used to the idea. By the time they returned to work on the following Monday, the idea had familiarity, credence – and acceptance.

10.   **Value**

Staff can only be expected to produce good and continuing high levels and quality of work, and continued commitment to their place of work, if they are as well paid and rewarded as possible. Low wages for low levels of commitment and hard work constitute a valueless, unproductive and, ultimately, destructive relationship (whatever the state of the labour market or numbers of unemployed). Low-level officials of the Communist Party in the

former USSR have their own proverbial version of this: 'We pretend to work, and they pretend to pay us.'

11.   The need to know

This is one of the most damaging and demoralizing of phrases. It is used by managers of organizations in describing the extent and volume of information that the rest of the staff are deemed to require. Organizations which take a prescriptive view of this demoralize and alienate the rest of their staff.

Protagonists of 'the need to know' approach cite commercial confidentiality as the overwhelming reason for it. On the one hand, plainly, organizations have to protect their commercial position. This has to be balanced against what a genuine business secret is. Very little that is described as such by such organizations has any impact on business performance once the particular information emerges. Genuine business secrets are few and far between as are genuine needs for confidentiality. This should always be limited to information about individuals or about a genuinely new invention.

12.   Mistakes and errors

This is a summary of two organizations' attitudes to mistakes and errors. It is taken from two consecutive items on the BBC Radio 4 'Today' programme in May 1996.

• Serious mismanagement and maladministration have come to light in a large government function. The person in charge was asked the following question.

    Interviewer: 'Do you think any mistakes were made and if so, what were they?'
    Response: 'There were no mistakes. Mistakes were not made.'

• A Japanese electrical goods giant had just won planning approval to extend and enlarge its factory site in the UK. This was going to lead to the creation of 1,400 new jobs. The person in charge was asked the following:

    Interviewer: 'So then – you don't make mistakes. You get everything right, first time, every time?'
    Response: 'Of course we make mistakes. I make them – lots of them – every day. The important thing – the reason why we are so successful – is that we acknowledge them and learn from them.'